SMARTER WORLD, BIGGER THREATS

Understanding the Internet of Things

ABDUL B. SUBHANI

AND

DR. MUHAMMAD FAISAL AMJAD

abbott press

This book is a work of non-fiction. Unless otherwise noted, the author and the publisher make no explicit guarantees as to the accuracy of the information contained in this book and in some cases, names of people and places have been altered to protect their privacy.

Abbott Press books may be ordered through booksellers or by contacting:

Abbott Press
1663 Liberty Drive
Bloomington, IN 47403
www.abbottpress.com
Phone: 1 (866) 697-5310

Because of the dynamic nature of the Internet, any web addresses or links contained in this book may have changed since publication and may no longer be valid. The views expressed in this work are solely those of the author and do not necessarily reflect the views of the publisher, and the publisher hereby disclaims any responsibility for them.

ISBN: 978-1-4582-2265-7 (sc)
ISBN: 978-1-4582-2264-0 (hc)
ISBN: 978-1-4582-2263-3 (e)

Library of Congress Control Number: 2020900633

Print information available on the last page.

Abbott Press rev. date: 1/24/2020

*Abdul B. Subhani dedicates this book
to his business partners:*

William Wallace Vernon
&
Emmadell Ewing Vernon

*Dr. Muhammad Faisal Amjad dedicates
this book to his family.*

Special Contributions by

Courtney Kissel
&
Bailey Martinez

Edited by
Kenyon Papillion

Contents

CHAPTER 1

Introduction to the Internet of Things

Forty Years of IT Revolution

The information technology revolution is regarded as one of mankind's major developments. The last forty-plus years have seen IT affect every facet of our lives, transforming the world into a place where automated processes and hyperconnected people and organizations are primary features. E-commerce has further turned the world into a global village, where the impact of globalization is seen in almost every aspect of our lives.

And yet, the IT revolution shows no signs of ending anytime soon. New dimensions to IT are still being discovered and researched. Recent developments have included the rise of social media, affecting not only people but also organizations and governments through the ability to form and modify public opinion. In addition, enhanced connectivity mechanisms have led to a new phenomenon—the online lifestyle, where staying online, always connected, has become common. The era of mobile computing has ushered in an age where virtual reality and the physical world converge. This convergence has already started playing itself out through the emergence of the Internet of Things (IoT).

1. Defining IoT

Because IoT is still in the early stages, no universally accepted definition currently exists. Examples of some proposed definitions include:

- "A system of interrelated computing devices, mechanical and digital machines, objects, animals or people that are provided with unique identifiers and the ability to transfer data over a network without requiring human-to-human or human-to-computer interaction."[1]
- "The ever-growing network of physical objects that feature an IP address for internet connectivity, and the communication that occurs between these objects and other Internet-enabled devices and systems."[2]
- "Sensors and actuators[3] embedded in physical objects … linked through wired and wireless networks, often using the same Internet Protocol (IP) that connects the Internet."[4]
- "The network of physical objects that contain embedded technology to communicate and sense or interact with their internal states or the external environment."[5]
- "The connection of devices (other than typical fare such as computers and smartphones) to the Internet. Cars, kitchen appliances, and even heart monitors can all be connected through the IoT … a network of internet-connected objects able to collect and exchange data using embedded sensors."[6]
- "A computing concept that describes the idea of everyday physical objects being connected to the internet and being able to identify themselves to other devices. The term is closely

---

[1] http://internetofthingsagenda.techtarget.com/definition/Internet-of-Things-IoT
[2] http://www.webopedia.com/TERM/I/internet_of_things.html
[3] Sensors are instruments that detect changes in an environment. Actuators are instruments that an object uses to make changes to an environment.
[4] https://iot-analytics.com/internet-of-things-definition/
[5] http://www.gartner.com/it-glossary/internet-of-things/
[6] http://www.businessinsider.com/what-is-the-internet-of-things-definition-2016-8

identified with RFID[7] as the method of communication, although it also may include other sensor technologies, wireless technologies or QR codes[8]." [9]

- "The interconnection via the Internet of computing devices embedded in everyday objects, enabling them to send and receive data."[10]

2. Key Features of IoT

Key concepts, features, and terminology of the IoT landscape can be extracted from the definitions presented above. All of the definitions mention a few general IoT imperatives, such as "devices," "sensors and actuators," "connectivity of devices," "internetworking," "exchange of data," "automated provision of the services," and "no or limited human interaction." Each of these imperatives is an important part of IoT, and each deserves to be considered in greater depth.

2.1 Devices Called *Things*

Devices, entities referred to as *things* in the term Internet of Things, include nearly any object that can provide some sort of service. The promise of IoT is that, someday, our daily interactions with such objects will be somewhat, if not fully, automated.

Common examples of *things* include refrigerators, security cameras, cars, and smart TVs. Transition into an IoT realm requires the gradual and phased transformation of our dumb devices into smart IoT things. Additionally, new *things* will be developed to natively link into IoT.

---

[7] Radio-frequency identification (RFID) uses radio waves to capture information stored in tags attached to objects.

[8] A type of matrix barcode

[9] https://www.techopedia.com/definition/28247/internet-of-things-iot

[10] https://en.oxforddictionaries.com/definition/Internet_of_things

2.2 Sensors and Actuators

Achieving automation through IoT requires automatic and spontaneous inputs with the help of sensors, which are instruments that detect changes in environments. While sensors provide IoT devices with the necessary inputs, actuators are the instruments that provide the output.

Already, the combination of sensors and actuators is common in devices. For example, sensors can be designed to determine the presence or absence of a food item in a refrigerator, sense the temperature in a home, or detect motion through a security camera. A smartphone camera senses light conditions and sets the flash to be either *on* or *off*. Automated garage door systems are another example of sensors combined with actuators to perform specific actions based on the type of input sensed by their receivers.

2.3 Connectivity of Devices

Connected devices are a fundamental requirement of IoT. A sophisticated device with enormous computing power and huge local storage remains limited in its capabilities if it is not connected to other devices. A disconnected device cannot be considered a *thing* in IoT.

Most of the network connectivity envisioned by IoT will likely be wireless, due to the size and distributed nature of IoT. Numerous wireless communication protocols are being developed to be capable of securely handling IoT's highly dynamic data streams.

2.4 Internetworking

Simply connecting devices is not enough; they must also be able to reliably internetwork. The deployment of the latest Internet protocol,[11] IPv6, allows billions of devices to simultaneously connect to the Internet. But this is only the beginning; even more lightweight

---

[11] Provides a standard of rules for sending and receiving data over the Internet.

protocols[12] are required for faster and more reliable communication, as Internet traffic from new, always *on*, and always communicating devices continues to increase.

2.5 Exchange of Information

Reliable information exchange is a fundamental requirement for automated decision-making processes. Ideally, devices should aggregate data from sensors and, using the network, send only the necessary information to the control system.

2.6 Automation of Processes and Services

IoT is expected to bring more automation to the workplace and to the home. The expected result is a future where devices are constantly sensing the environment for automatic inputs rather than waiting for human input. A typical example of such automation is a smart refrigerator sensing the shortage of milk and ordering it online, all without human involvement.

Closely linked with the objective of automated processes, is the goal of an automated service provision model. Consider the same example of the smart refrigerator filling itself up with required groceries. The grocery store provides the service of making utility items available on a daily basis. At present, these services may not be automatic, meaning human action is likely required. However, IoT is expected to provide such services automatically by sensing human needs and environments.

2.7 Limited or no Human Involvement

An expected outcome of automated processes and services is a reduced role for human input in repetitive processes. Similarly, expanding IoT is also expected to diminish the role of the supply chain middleman.

---

[12] A communication protocol with less complexity in order to reduce resources needed to perform some task.

3. An Example *Thing* in IoT

In her article "What Makes Up the Internet of Things?" Dr. Irena Bojanova uses the example of a smart car as a *thing* that is a part of IoT.[13] A smart car uses multiple Internet-accessible sensors and actuators to gain information about changes in its environment.

For example, a GPS sensor would collect location data, and the speedometer would know the instantaneous speed of the vehicle. Other sensors can be included in components, such as the suspension, airbags, emissions, skid, and collision mechanisms.

Actuators would be the instruments or parts that the *thing* uses to impact the environment. For example, through the brake controller, the vehicle can decelerate. Other actuators can be the throttle controller, stability controller, windshield wipers, etc.

4. History of IoT

Discovering the potential future of IoT first requires understanding its history. By understanding technological trends and past developments, we have some basis for making predictions about future trends or developments rather than just guessing.

4.1 Embedded Systems and Pervasive Computing

Embedded systems are combinations of hardware and software that are designed to carry out a certain task or tasks. They rely on custom-built computers or microcontrollers to perform this dedicated set of tasks. These systems have been around since the 1970s. Embedded computers are lightweight and smaller in size compared to general-purpose computers. They also consume less power and are, therefore,

---

[13] https://www.computer.org/portal/web/sensing-iot/content?g=53926943&type=article&urlTitle=what-are-the-components-of-iot-

cheaper. Examples of embedded systems include digital watches, calculators, and traffic light systems.

Pervasive computing, also sometimes called ubiquitous computing, refers to the trend of embedding computers in devices. Pervasive computing uses microcontrollers in devices to automate the devices' tasks with limited or no interaction by the end user. Generally, pervasive computing devices are networked and are always online. IoT is the next generation of pervasive computing.

4.2 The Term "Internet of Things"

In 1999, while Kevin Ashton was working at Procter & Gamble, he tried to draw management's attention toward RFID technology for supply chain optimization. He referred to his presentation as "Internet of Things," as he explained in 2009:[14]

> I could be wrong, but I'm fairly sure the phrase "Internet of Things" started life as the title of a presentation I made at Procter & Gamble (P&G) in 1999. Linking the new idea of RFID in P&G's supply chain to the then-red-hot topic of the Internet was more than just a good way to get executive attention. It summed up an important insight—one that 10 years later, after the Internet of Things has become the title of everything from an article in Scientific American to the name of a European Union conference, is still often misunderstood. The fact that I was probably the first person to say "Internet of Things" doesn't give me any right to control how others use the phrase. But what I meant, and still mean, is this: Today computers—and, therefore, the Internet—are almost wholly dependent on human beings for information. Nearly all of the roughly 50 petabytes (a petabyte is 1,024 terabytes) of

---

[14] Ashton, Kevin. "That 'Internet of Things' Thing," *RFiD Journal* 22.7 (2009): 97–114.

data available on the Internet were first captured and created by human beings—by typing, pressing a record button, taking a digital picture or scanning a bar code. Conventional diagrams of the Internet include servers and routers and so on, but they leave out the most numerous and important routers of all: people. The problem is, people have limited time, attention and accuracy—all of which means they are not very good at capturing data about things in the real world.

4.3 Into the Twenty-First Century

In a 1999 article for *Businessweek*, Professor Neil Gross predicted what IoT would look like in the twenty-first century.[15] He put it as follows:

> In the next century, planet earth will don an electronic skin. It will use the Internet as a scaffold to support and transmit its sensations. This skin is already being stitched together. It consists of millions of embedded electronic measuring devices: thermostats, pressure gauges, pollution detectors, cameras, microphones, glucose sensors, EKGs, electroencephalographs. These will probe and monitor cities and endangered species, the atmosphere, our ships, highways and fleets of trucks, our conversations, our bodies—even our dreams.

From this point, Postscapes continues tracking the history of IoT developments by manufacturers around the world.[16] Notable highlights from this history include the following:

- **2000**
  - o LG announced its plans to manufacture Internet refrigerators.

---

[15] https://www.bloomberg.com/news/articles/1999-08-29/14-the-earth-will-don-an-electronic-skin

[16] https://www.postscapes.com/internet-of-things-history/

- **2002–04**
  - o The term *Internet of Things* was already receiving attention in popular publication journals and research work.[17]
  - o RFID also was rapidly becoming part of many projects.
- **2005**
  - o The International Telecommunications Union (ITU) published its first report on IoT.[18] The report covered the concept of IoT, associated technologies, expected market opportunities, challenges related to IoT, and implications for the developing world.
- **2008**
  - o The first European IoT Conference, the International Conference for Industry and Academia, was held in Zurich.[19]
  - o The IPSO Alliance[20] began encouraging the use of IP networks for smart objects to promote IoT.[21]
  - o The US National Intelligence Council included IoT in its list of the top six disruptive civil technologies[22] that would impact US interests in the near future.[23]
- **2010**
  - o China declared IoT a key industry when Premier Wen Jiabao identified IoT as an emerging strategic industry in an interview with state media.[24]

---

[17] https://www.forbes.com/global/2002/0318/092.html#5242d5b83c3e; Eero Huvio, John Grönvall, Kary Främling, "Tracking and Tracing Parcels Using a Distributed Computing Approach," In: SOLEM, Olav (ed.) Proceedings of the 14th Annual Conference for Nordic Researchers in Logistics (NOFOMA'2002), Trondheim, Norway, June 12–14, 2002. pp. 29–43.

[18] http://www.itu.int/osg/spu/publications/internetofthings/InternetofThings_summary.pdf

[19] http://www.the-internet-of-things.org/iot2008/

[20] An organization dedicated to promoting the Internet of Things.

[21] https://www.ipso-alliance.org/about-us/

[22] These are technologies that the US National Intelligence Council believes have the potential to increase or decrease US power over the next fifteen-year period.

[23] https://www.dni.gov/index.php

[24] https://readwrite.com/2010/01/19/chinese_premier_internet_of_things/

Since 2010, IoT has been further developed and continues to evolve through research, industrial development, and standardization.

5. Understanding IoT

IoT has spent some time in development within the overall IT industry. IoT emerged out of the recent quest for automation, extensive mobile computing, and a hyperconnected lifestyle.

5.1 Automation

One of the most notable effects of the IT revolution in daily life is the automation of processes and services. For example, automatic bill pay and automated customer service are both services that most adults in the developed world have had experience with. As IT continues to advance, manual and mechanical systems seem to be fading away. While manpower and human intelligence can never completely vanish, recent years have seen quite a few advancements curtailing traditional human roles.

The race to an automated way of life has been one of the primary drivers of IoT—a realm where processes and routes can be further shortened and accelerated. For example, although we already embrace online shopping, we still anticipate a day when the shopping process is even further automated, such as a refrigerator sensing a shortage of milk and automatically ordering more.

5.2 Mobile Computing

With the rise of mobile devices over the last decade, people are just as likely to use a mobile device to access the Internet as a desktop computer. In fact, in 2016, mobile and tablet device Internet usage accounted for 51.3 percent of all Internet usage, surpassing desktop Internet usage for the first time.[25] Static systems are mostly limited to corporate environments,

---

[25] http://gs.statcounter.com/press/mobile-and-tablet-internet-usage-exceeds-desktop-for-first-time-worldwide

academia, and research facilities. By contrast, individuals are getting more used to carrying their computing and storage devices with them at all times, rather than relying on a desktop computer.

Mobility in IT has created an expectation that IT should be available everywhere we go. Appliances must have processing capabilities with storage so that they can make decisions. We now expect the ability to control our environments with just a tap on our mobile devices.

5.3 Hyperconnectivity

Online profiles are regularly and constantly updated with people's interests, including entertainment, business, or social connections. Ensuring these constant updates occur requires a constant Internet connection. Gone are the days when people would look around for Internet hotspots. Now, every mobile service provider also offers Internet connectivity services. New homes are built with network connectivity built within the walls, and open areas are lit with Wi-Fi coverage. These advances exist and converge to grant ubiquitous connectivity.

With this connectivity, we expect to be connected not just to each other, but also to our "things," such as security cameras or air conditioning systems. Furthermore, we want our devices networked together in order to autonomously complete various tasks. For example, we might want our cars to set up an oil change appointment with a mechanic as soon as they sense a change is needed. Or we might want garbage trucks to pick up trash only when our garbage bins are full rather than according to some predetermined schedule.

5.4 Increasing Bandwidth

Increased bandwidth has been a major factor in the Internet's growth over the last few decades. People used to rely on modems and telephone lines for Internet service. The narrow bandwidth offered by these methods meant that content download or upload took a long time. The lack of bandwidth meant the Internet's backbone could not handle bandwidth-intensive applications and services, such as video streaming. The Internet's infrastructure was also not good enough for billions of devices to connect to it simultaneously.

Later years saw rapid advancements in the field of digital communications, including T1 lines and, later, digital subscriber lines (DSL), with greater bandwidth. Subsequently, wave division multiplexing coupled with fiber optic technology enhanced available bandwidth to new, much higher levels.

Wireless networking, although not very widespread in the beginning due to security concerns, also made substantial improvements in both security and reach, enhancing and ensuring Internet access for end users at the higher bandwidth levels. The flourishing of smartphones and mobile computing during the same period was also affected by increased bandwidth availability.

Today, the Internet's robust network infrastructure, wide backbone, and extended reach allow it to host billions of new devices. Supporting even more devices, as anticipated with IoT, will require even more infrastructure and bandwidth. However, if growth continues at the same pace, these enhancements will soon emerge through continued research and development.[26]

5.5 Cloud Computing

In the early years of the IT revolution, local storage was costly. It was only in the era of personal, desktop computers (PCs) that local hard disk became an exciting, relevant feature. Local storage size increased rapidly and exponentially, alongside the processing power of PCs. By the start of the twenty-first century, powerful PCs were equipped with huge amounts of processing power and local storage capacities.[27]

---

[26] From 1983 to 2018, bandwidth grew by more than 50 percent per year. This is sometimes known as Nielsen's Law. *See* https://www.nngroup.com/articles/law-of-bandwidth/.

[27] https://www.computerhistory.org/timeline/computers/

Cloud computing, the trend of using servers on the Internet for data storage, processing, and management, has now gained a foothold in IT. Many cloud computing service models have emerged, including software as a service (SaaS), platform as a service (PaaS) and infrastructure as a service (IaaS). Various cloud computing deployment models, such as private cloud, public cloud, and hybrid cloud, have also been implemented.

5.6 Miniaturization

Miniaturization is responsible for much of IoT's enabling technologies. In the initial days of IT, a mainframe computer was housed in a medium-sized room. However, moving from vacuum tubes to transistors, then to very large scale integration (VLSI) and microprocessors, allowed miniaturization to occur. Still, even smaller-sized gadgets with more processing power and larger storage capacities continue to be produced. Computers in wristwatches, projectors and cameras in smartphones, and slim display devices are the results of miniaturization. Today, miniaturization seems to show no signs of slowing down.[28]

6. Terms Related to IoT

As the discussion around IoT has grown, multiple terms, such as *Internet of Everything (IoE)*, *Web of Things*, *Machine to Machine (M2M) Communication*, *Industrial Internet*, and *Industry 4.0* have been suggested as somehow synonymous with IoT. However, each of these terms has a different meaning from IoT.

- **Internet of Everything (IoE).** IoE aims to encompass IoT, and it may be the term closest to synonymous with IoT. IoE encompasses all connections and entities that can communicate over Internet connections.

---

[28] https://www.forbes.com/sites/startswithabang/2018/03/08/breakthrough-in-miniaturized-inductors-to-revolutionize-electronics/#76f9609c779e

- **Web of Things**. Unlike IoT, the term *Web of Things* covers only the World Wide Web, meaning the connectivity it references includes only software web applications.
- **Machine to Machine (M2M)**. M2M is a telecommunications buzzword implying wired and wireless networks of all sorts of devices.
- **Industrial Internet**. *Industrial Internet* refers to the interaction of networking hardware technologies with applications and services. The industrial Internet "draws together fields such as machine learning, big data, the Internet of things and machine-to-machine communication to ingest data from machines, analyze it (often in real-time), and use it to adjust operations."[29]
- **Industry 4.0**. *Industry 4.0* envisions a new industrial revolution that computerizes the manufacturing industry. A synonymous term is *smart factory*, due to the potential benefits for the industrial development.

IoT Analytics illustrates the scope and relationship of the above terms with the following figure:[30]

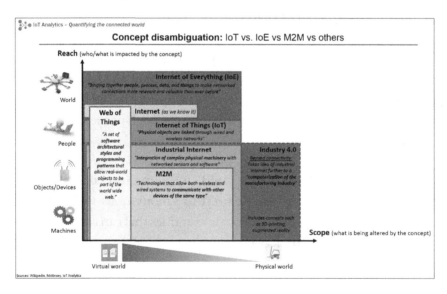

---

[29] http://www.industrialinternet.us/revive/

[30] https://iot-analytics.com/internet-of-things-definition/

7. IoT Benefits

IoT has the potential to bring about many positive changes to people's lives by making their lives simpler and less stressful. Even now, in its infancy, IoT is demonstrating potential benefits that are likely to grow as it expands.

7.1 Automation

Automation is the foremost benefit of IoT. IoT is expected to usher in an era of automatic decisions made by devices and things to facilitate daily life. For example, mobile phones will tell home automation systems to turn on the lights and air conditioning, open the garage door, and prepare a cup of coffee at the preferred temperature by the user's expected arrival time.

7.2 Efficient Data Collection and Instant Access

Today's business world relies heavily on data pertaining to user experiences, likes, and dislikes. Supply chain management systems are also highly dependent on the flow of information. IoT would automate these data exchanges. Moreover, the amount of data gathered by huge numbers of things and sensors would significantly increase. However, with the help of intelligent systems, this data would be instantly converted into useful information and accessible from anywhere.

7.3 Shared Awareness

Huge data coupled with efficient data mining tools enables decision-makers to get the best value out of the shared awareness made available through IoT.

7.4 Improved Customer Engagement

IoT can help businesses actively engage with customers. Businesses can learn about customer likes and dislikes by analyzing data received from

IoT devices. By understanding how customers use their IoT devices, businesses can tailor their processes to meet those preferences. This has the potential for greater customer satisfaction and retention—ultimately resulting in a boost to the business's bottom line.

7.5 Technology Optimization

Aside from improved customer experience, the rapid feedback in the form of user data, offered by IoT will also result in technological improvements and optimization. Reaping IoT's full benefits will require technology to continually evolve—becoming better, cheaper, and safer.

7.6 Cost Savings

Smart cities and smart grids are examples of IoT applications that will result in huge cost savings by improving the reliability and efficiency of energy grids.[31] IoT deployment is also expected to create similar decreases in power consumption, reliance on fossil fuel, vehicle accidents, traffic congestion, pollution, and healthcare complications.

7.7 Waste Reduction

Decisions based on delayed data collection can lead to wasted resources and efforts (e.g., trying to complete a task that someone else has already completed). However, IoT is expected to bring real-time information at all times. As a result, wasted time, money, and manpower are expected to decrease as IoT deployment increases.

8. IoT Risks and Complications

All new technologies come with risks; IoT is no exception. Early identification of associated risks is essential to prepare for potential problems and provides time to plan countermeasures.

---

[31] https://www.juniperresearch.com/press/press-releases/smart-grids-to-save-city-dwellers-$14bn-in-energy

8.1 Security

Security is the topmost risk with IoT. Compromised IoT security is already making headlines. Last year saw some devastating DDoS attacks take advantage of IoT devices. Attacks like these, ranging in magnitude from 620 Gbps[32] to around 1 Tbps,[33] had never been seen before.[34]

Too many insecure IoT devices in the market made it easy for attackers to infect and turn them into zombies as part of a huge botnet.[35] This botnet was employed to launch massive DDoS attacks against companies and their services.

However, this does not mean that IoT is doomed before even taking off. The reason for such insecurities is that, as in other areas of IT, security has been treated as an afterthought. Manufacturers are in a hurry to bring their IoT products into the market to avoid being left behind. Additionally, IoT has widened the overall attack surface offered to attackers. The huge number of IoT devices coupled with a massive repository of data creates a giant target that must be protected.

Another aspect of IoT that makes security more difficult is the fact that IoT devices have limited storage and computational capabilities. This resource-constrained nature of IoT devices makes implementing sophisticated security solutions almost impossible.

---

[32] Gigabytes per second.

[33] Terabytes per second.

[34] *See* https://krebsonsecurity.com/2016/09/krebsonsecurity-hit-with-record-ddos/; https://www.ovh.com/us/news/articles/a2367.the-ddos-that-didnt-break-the-camels-vac; http://hub.dyn.com/static/hub.dyn.com/dyn-blog/dyn-statement-on-10-21-2016-ddos-attack.html.

[35] A collection of Internet-connected devices that are infected with malware and controlled by an attacker.

8.2 Privacy

Closely linked with security is the issue of privacy. Smartphones, tablets, desktops, and laptops used to be the only devices online with data exposure risks. However, IoT promises that home appliances, healthcare devices, and consumer equipment will all be online as well. IoT devices are intended to constantly collect personal information for shared awareness and informed decision-making and to store the collected data in the cloud. This raises serious doubts about the industry's ability to properly handle such private data because the IT industry is already unable to satisfy customers' data privacy concerns in non-IoT environments.

8.3 Standardization and Compliance

IoT suffers from a lack of standardization. Already, with proprietary technologies as a common feature, many IoT products are incompatible with other devices or underlying platforms. Therefore, there is a risk that consumers will purchase IoT devices which do not function in the way in which they should. By standardizing the technology associated with various IoT devices, the risk of these incompatibility issues will decrease.

8.4 Unemployment

Unfortunately, as IoT takes off, employment prospects for humans are expected to suffer. With IoT managing buyer/seller relationships more quickly and with much less friction, the middleman will likely be eliminated. For example, if manufacturers could more accurately gauge consumer demand by using IoT data, some retailers and wholesalers could be eliminated from the buying/selling process. Additionally, the extensive automation of smart homes and smart cities is also expected to take its toll on the role of manpower.

8.5 Complexity

IoT promises cultural change affecting every walk of life. Even in its current state of limited deployment, complexity is evident in the form of interoperability[36] and connectivity issues. Yet, the actual complexity of IoT in the wake of full rollout is impossible to envision. Compatibility problems, software patches, update management, network congestion, and user rights management can turn into highly complex matters as IoT expands.

8.6 Data Storage

With IoT's huge number of devices constantly generating vast quantities of sensing and control data, the need of data storage space is expected to grow significantly. Additionally, this need for data storage is also expected to grow for efficient techniques to retrieve and utilize the data.

9. Standardization Concerns

As interest in IoT grows, the IT industry has felt an urgency to produce IoT-related solutions, hardware, and software. However, the rapid pace of these developments has resulted in a clear lack of standardization and consistency. Consequently, compatibility issues are quite common in the IoT world. The need for a standardized model for common IoT initiatives cannot be overemphasized.

9.1 Need for Standardization

Ahmed Banafa, in his article "IoT Standardization and Implementation Challenges," identifies four categories for IoT standardization.[37]

---

[36] The ability of different devices to connect and work together to complete some task.
[37] https://ahmedbanafa.blogspot.com/2016/10/iot-standardization-and-implementation.html

- **Platform.** This is the underlying layer where huge volumes of data flow take place. Model analysis tools and protocols at this level are critical.
- **Connectivity.** This is the area where the end user enters the IoT realm with smart devices (wearable, smart cars, smart appliances, etc.). Scalable and seamless connectivity is the critical need at this level.
- **Business Model.** A set of models for initiating an IoT business motivates both new startups and seasoned veterans. Different models may be tailored for various business types.
- **Applications.** IoT application development must have a blueprint to ensure interoperability and compatibility. Actions like controlling devices and sensors, data acquisition and processing, analysis, and decision-making should all be standardized.

9.2 Standard Bodies

Several standard bodies are already working on IoT streamlining. However, each body has its own scope of work and objectives.

- **IEEE Standard for an Architectural Framework for IoT.** This group endeavors to support cross-domain collaboration among various stakeholders, assist in interoperability of systems, and enhance compatibility in functionality under the umbrella of IoT.[38]
- **The Industrial Internet Consortium (IIC).** Rather than an initiative directed toward technical design aspects like protocols and standards, IIC supports the industrial world in IoT-related progress by creating testbeds (platform used to test a technology) and use cases (describes how a person uses a system to achieve a particular goal).[39]

---

[38] https://standards.ieee.org/develop/project/2413.html
[39] http://www.iiconsortium.org/

- **Open Connectivity Foundation (OCF).** OCF is focused on attaining interoperability in a secure fashion for end users, enterprises, and industry by presenting a common communications ground, and an open-source implementation, allowing entities to collaborate irrespective of specifications.[40]
- **Thread.** The goal of this group is to create a networking protocol based on IPv6 that would enable IoT devices to discover and connect with each other.[41]
- **AllSeen Alliance.** This industrial group works to enable the interoperability of IoT devices, services, and applications.[42]

Conclusion

Understanding IoT's basic concepts is important before diving deep into its security realm. In many ways, IoT is a physical extension of the Internet beyond computing machines like desktop, laptops, and mobile devices. IoT seeks to bring everything onto the global network.

While the Internet remains a multipurpose world for many services and applications covering various areas of interest, IoT focuses on automating procedures and systems through shared awareness and intelligence. IoT has been in the rollout phase for quite some time. Expectations are high and the pace of progress is rapid. While there are still many apprehensions regarding issues such as security, standardization, and privacy, IoT also has the potential to introduce many new benefits and opportunities.

---

[40] https://openconnectivity.org/
[41] http://www.threadgroup.org/
[42] http://www.allseenalliance.org/

CHAPTER 2

IoT Architecture and Design

IoT Perspectives

Before diving into IoT security challenges, it is imperative to acquire basic knowledge of IoT design principles, constituent components, and functional architecture. There are three perspectives through which we can view IoT: IoT as layers, IoT as functions, and IoT as components. Additionally, specific types of hardware design and software development are needed to make IoT possible. Basic knowledge of these perspectives and features will help us to better understand the particular vulnerabilities associated with IoT technology.

1. IoT as Layers

The first perspective through which to view IoT is in the form of layers. These layers are hierarchical, have separate functions, and each layer interacts with the layers above and/or below it.

1.1 The Network Layer (The Connectivity Plane)

IoT is developed on top of the *network layer*, or *connectivity plane*. Interestingly, most of the elements required for the network layer already exist in the form of the Internet's network architecture, including Internet protocols (IP) and the lower layers of the Internet protocol suite (TCP/IP) stack. The Internet still needs to grow manyfold to host all of the coming IoT infrastructure. However, its presence provides a basic platform upon which IoT can grow nonstop, rather than having to build this layer from scratch. The first step in creating this growth is shifting to IPv6 because a much greater number of IP addresses is needed for the expected increase of the number of IoT devices. Another step is to continually add more infrastructure to the network layer.

1.2 The Things Layer (IoT Devices)

The layer above the network layer is where the specific IoT entities reside. Devices in the *things layer* all require the network layer below to provide them with the necessary connectivity and bandwidth. While the network layer has to seamlessly host these entities, the things layer must allow the IoT devices—smart refrigerators, trash bins, ovens, etc.—to continuously share information with each other, or with the central control. In addition to their primary functions, these devices are embedded with sensors to gain information for automated decision-making or intelligence, such as a wearable IoT device with the ability to sense health conditions. Continuous data input from these sensors must be stored, preferably with cloud storage on the network layer.

1.3 The Interfaces and Active Engagement Layer

The final layer, the *interfaces and active engagement layer*, allows the IoT device to interact with the real world. End users, user facilities, or environmental conditions must be able to provide necessary input, gain some processed output, or exchange control messages through these interfaces. For example, if you told your smart home to turn on your bedroom lights, your verbal command would be the necessary input and the smart home actually turning on the lights would be the processed output.

2. IoT as Functions

IoT can also be viewed as consisting of several functional elements. These functional elements work together to provide the services that we expect from IoT. They include the following:

2.1 Connectivity

The *connectivity framework* is the platform on which IoT-enabled devices reside. As a functional component of the IoT big picture, connectivity allows devices to communicate and exchange data to work as a system.

2.2 Devices and Sensors

Billions of devices including sensing systems are the main utility of IoT and provide its most prominent functionality.

2.3 Intelligence

IoT devices not only sense; they also add value to the collected data through the ability to make efficient decisions. For example, a smart refrigerator that orders a food item when it notices that it is low is analyzing data and then making a decision based on that data. It is performing intelligently in the same way that a human who notices something decides to act based on that information.

2.4 Active Engagement

IoT devices are designed to always be available for user interaction. They are always online and continuously sharing information with their control mechanisms in order to provide users with real-time services.

3. IoT as Components

A third way of describing IoT is by listing the constituent components of today's IoT landscape. These components are just the individual parts of the IoT landscape. They include the following:

3.1 Physical Objects

Physical objects, also known as *things* in the IoT environment, are the instruments that sense the physical world and use the collected data for informed decision-making.

3.2 Sensors

Embedded within the physical objects, sensors monitor the environment and convert environmental changes into digital signals for generating effects in the IoT system.

3.3 Actuators

Actuators within a physical object are the output modules that execute the decisions reached by the IoT system and take action to affect the physical environment.

3.4 Virtual Entities

Although virtual entities have no physical existence, they are an important part of the overall IoT system. Examples such as cryptocurrency, bitcoin, electronic wallets, e-tickets, etc., already play a growing role in ecommerce and in IoT.

3.5 People

As users of the IoT landscape, people are also IoT components. As IoT becomes more of a necessity, like today's Internet and World Wide Web, the role of almost all human beings as part of the IoT system will continue to increase.

3.6 Services

IoT is all about facilitating service providers and service seekers for e-commerce, travel, consumer services, and related industries. Services in IoT are available through the network and shared among similar devices through cloud services.

3.7 Platforms

Platforms, or *frameworks*, support various IoT device functionalities, such as software upgrades. Platforms make the operation of IoT devices similar, coherent, and efficient.

3.8 Network

The network architecture supporting the IoT world provides connectivity, wired or wireless, through many different technologies and topologies. Without network connectivity, IoT cannot be realized. All IoT protocols and services come over the network.

4. IoT Hardware Design

Daniel Elizalde, in his article "IoT Hardware—Introduction and Explanation," explains the building blocks of an IoT device.[43] In the article, he gives an overview of the hardware that is important for IoT development and technology.

4.1 The *Thing* Itself

This is the physical entity, such as a car or a refrigerator, that is required to be brought into the IoT domain as an IoT device. IoT devices can be objects specially designed for IoT or existing devices slightly modified to form part of IoT.

---

[43] https://iot-for-all.com/iot-hardware-introduction-explanation/

4.2 Data Acquisition Module

This hardware part uses one or more sensors to convert physical information into digital signals. These digital signals are then forwarded to a computing module for data processing.

4.3 Data Processing Module

This piece of hardware uses input from the sensors, after necessary conversion to digital format, to process all the sensory data in real time. In many cases, the data processing module is assisted by local storage on the edge IoT device. The size of local storage depends on how much data must be retained on the edge device.

4.4 Communication Module

The communication module is responsible for information exchange among the IoT entities and between the IoT entities and the cloud. Every IoT device requires a built-in interface for network connectivity.

5. IoT Software Development

The design and development of IoT software requires specific skills. IoT software development calls for a skillset involving embedded programming, middleware, lower layers of networking, associated frameworks, etc.

IoT software development aims to address functions like data collection, multiple device integration, real-time analysis, and application/process extension within the overall network architecture.

5.1 Data Collection and Distribution

IoT software must be developed to collect data in real time without errors. Data collection software modules should be designed for precise sensing, correct measurement, data filtering, and efficient integration.

Coupled with data collection is data distribution, which is the same process but in reverse. Control messages like configuration settings or even simple data transfers in real time are passed from the controlling mechanism to the end devices.

5.2 Hardware Integration

IoT aims to integrate devices into an active system. Without proper device integration, the concept of IoT lacks depth. The process of automation and machine decision-making comes only after seamless hardware integration. For an IoT environment to function efficiently, seamless and stable networking software is needed. Device integration software also requires appropriate, lightweight communication protocols.

5.3 Real-Time Analysis

Constantly generated data by billions of devices would be chaos if not managed properly. Huge data is of no use unless it is filtered, analyzed, and managed for timely decision-making. Thus, the IoT landscape relies heavily on software code that can analyze the flux of data in real time. Automated actions can be of value only if they are based on efficient and timely analytics.

5.4 Objective-Oriented Extension

IoT software must expand the reach of its hardware to increase its scope for a more effective and efficient system. The software should be able to mix and merge existing and new systems together as one unit when needed. Because IoT software is widely deployed, it should be scalable enough to avoid redeployment in case of minor changes in hardware scenarios.

Conclusion

IoT can be understood from a variety of perspectives, based on layers, functions, components, hardware, and software. Properly understanding IoT security aspects requires first understanding each of these perspectives and how they interact to form a more complete picture of the Internet of Things.

CHAPTER 3

IoT Security Challenges

Introduction

Security is the biggest concern for experts regarding IoT. The massive networking, enormous scope, and state of hyperconnectivity promised by IoT make it a lucrative playground for hackers and cybercriminals.

IoT faces major information security challenges, especially related to the confidentiality, integrity, and availability triad. Properly dealing with these challenges requires understanding the IoT threat environment. The vulnerabilities of upcoming systems, the risks associated with widespread IoT adoption, and the stakes of entities involved with whole IoT landscape all take part in shaping this threat environment. Security controls and mechanisms must be implemented into the IoT landscape to meet these challenges.

1. Significance of Information Security

Information security can be understood as the measures taken to ensure the protection of data from outsiders while allowing insiders reasonably easy access on a need-to-know basis. Information security requires thorough planning before implementation and continuous updating after implementation.

Security aspects cannot be overlooked when discussing new IT advancements, such as hyperconnectivity and IoT. The following key information security aspects should be researched for any new technology prior to that technology's release.

1.1 Defining the Threat Environment

Potential security compromises (*threats*) along with entities that exploit vulnerabilities and security lapses (*threat agents*) make up the *threat environment*. Understanding a system's threat environment, including the relevant threat agents and threats, is critical before the system can be properly secured.

1.2 Connecting Vulnerabilities and Risks

Vulnerabilities are lapses or weaknesses in a system that can lead to a security compromise. Many times, vulnerabilities exist due to a system's own peculiarities or work processes. While it is next to impossible to design a system without any vulnerabilities, the vulnerabilities that do exist in a system must be identified and addressed.

In the realm of information security, *risk* is the possibility that some threat agent might exploit a vulnerability. This exploit would then compromise a system, entirely or partially. Risk is calculated by estimating the impact that the losses from a compromise may cause to the system.

1.3 Identifying Assets

Assets are anything of value to the system or organization. An asset's importance can be ascertained in terms of its economic value, which may be its purchase cost, the impact cost due to its presence, or its loss cost due to its destruction or compromise. For example, think of a building. Its purchase cost would be what the building is bought for. Its impact cost would be how its presence affects the value of assets around it. And its loss cost would be how its absence affects the value of assets around it. Once assets have been identified and classified as per their value, they can be properly protected against threats by using control measures.

1.4 Deciding to Control: Safeguard or Counter

Controls, which include safeguards[44] and countermeasures,[45] bridge security gaps in order to prevent a threat agent from taking advantage of a vulnerability, thereby avoiding potential loss. Controls are placed after a thorough planning process involving threat assessment and risk management.

1.5 Transferring Information Security Principles to an IoT Environment

After understanding the key terminologies described above, the next step is to understand how all these aspects function in an IoT environment.

Consider an IoT-enabled access control system in which various security cameras are equipped with motion sensors record videos. These recordings are stored in a central repository in public cloud storage for viewing by an administrator. However, the organization has not purchased encrypted storage (likely due to the additional cost involved), meaning the data is unencrypted in the public cloud. A hacker then penetrates the cloud storage and steals the recorded videos.

In this case, the hacker is a threat agent. The threat is the possibility of data exposure. Risk is the envisioned loss if the asset—the video data—is exposed. The unencrypted storage is the vulnerability.

---

[44] Controls applied before the fact to prevent loss. Safeguards are proactive.

[45] Controls applied, when a safeguard fails, to prevent further loss. Countermeasures are reactive.

The organization could have employed better security through the safeguard of encrypting the data.

2. The CIA Triad

The crux of information security is the concept of the CIA triad: *confidentiality*, *integrity*, and *availability*. Before discussing IoT security challenges, it is important to have a basic understanding of this triad.

2.1 Confidentiality

Confidentiality is the principle of sharing information only on a need-to-know basis. When information is shared with only the relevant people, only those necessary individuals will have the ability to perform some action based on the information. For example, highly sensitive information should be accessible to fewer people than more general information. Confidentiality is all about classifying data as per roles and responsibilities.

Confidentiality is most needed for military and government organizations, where critical, sensitive information must not be shared with people who are not directly concerned. Confidentiality is also important for businesses, such as when a new project or product is concealed until the time it is ready for final launch. Exposure of an enterprise's trade secrets can be disastrous for productivity.

A crude way of attaining confidentiality is through a mechanism of usernames, passwords, and access control lists (ACL). In this case, sensitive information is password protected. Only people directly concerned with that information should be able to access it with their passwords. This mechanism can be further strengthened by defining strong password rules and employing two-factor authentication. Two-factor authentication normally combines what one possesses (such as biometric data or some physical object) with what one knows (i.e., the password) and then authorizes access to the restricted data or resource.

Examples of biometric data utilized include fingerprints, iris scans, and facial recognition.

Cryptography can also be used to achieve confidentiality of information. Classified information is encrypted, and those authorized to access it are given a decryption key to decipher that information and use it. For example, IoT devices collecting data from the environment may encrypt the data before sending it to the controlling entity. The controlling entity has the decryption key for the data and can use it to utilize the data.

Predefined rulesets, protocols, and standards should be agreed to by all parties in order to ensure similar kinds of confidentiality arrangements. One example is data exchange encryption through secure socket layers/transport layer security (SSL/TLS) protocols.

As IoT is being established, confidentiality plays a critical role. The huge number of entities expected to continuously generate and exchange data demand procedures ensuring that knowledge is shared only on a need-to-know basis. Access to the IoT devices, data exchange sessions between devices, cloud storage, control signals, etc., should all be classified.

2.2 Integrity

Another key element of information security is integrity. In other words, secured data must always be trustworthy and incapable of modification without authorization. However, integrity not only includes the trustworthiness of the data content, it also requires that the source generating or sending the data is accurate and reliable. Content trustworthiness is called *data integrity*, whereas origin trustworthiness is called *origin integrity* or *authentication*. The credibility of the data source has a direct effect on the integrity of the content. For example, otherwise factual news may be discounted if the reporting source is unauthentic, of low credibility, or from an anonymous source.

Implementing integrity as part of information security requires a mechanism to prevent any compromises of data integrity or data origin and another mechanism aimed at detecting any attempts at integrity compromise. While detection mechanisms do not stop data modification attempts, they do keep the data under constant watch and are prepared to report any instabilities.

Various mechanisms ensure data integrity during transmission and storage. For example, checksums, error detection and correction mechanisms, hash functions, etc., are useful for assuring data integrity.

For data origin authenticity, digital signatures are a common method. First, an entity initiating a message encrypts it with its own private key. Then, at the receiving end, the message must be decrypted with the public key of the sender. This ensures that the receiver knows who sent the message.

2.3 Availability

While information must be kept secure from negative forces, the information should also be available to those who are authorized. The mechanisms that ensure confidentiality and integrity should not make information unusable or inaccessible for legitimate users. Additionally, some malicious parties attempt to deny information access to legitimate users. Ensuring that information is always accessible by legitimate users is the underlying principle of availability.

An unavailable system or a piece of information is as good as no system or information at all. For example, if an error or attack makes an airline's IT network unavailable, IT-related tasks, such as customers booking flights or staff issuing new tickets, will come to a halt. The cumulative impact would be similar to a physical disaster incapacitating the airline.

Availability compromises due to errors, attacks, or natural disasters are more devastating for systems with greater dependence on IT services.

Therefore, availability is especially critical in an IoT environment. The future IoT landscape is predicted to be an era where every walk of life is dependent on data generated by IoT devices. If that data is unavailable, it becomes useless for intelligence and the active engagement necessary for IoT to function. Concepts designed to ensure availability, such as hyperconnectivity, cloud storage, and maintaining an underlying network, all play a dominant role in the success of IoT.

3. The IoT Threat Environment

Identifying the challenges IoT faces today first requires understanding the relevant threat environment. By reviewing past experiences and then reshaping the attack vectors, a threat assessment can evaluate trending attacks on IoT-enabled technologies. As a result of this assessment, IoT's extended attack surface, cyberterrorism, large-scale distributed denial of service (DDoS) attacks, massive ransomware, widespread malware attacks, and privacy threats have already been identified as primary concerns for IoT.

3.1 Attack Surface Extension

Every system has weak or less protected areas called *vulnerabilities* where an attack can be perpetrated. The route an attacker uses to access the target system by exploiting vulnerabilities is called an *attack vector*. Multiple attack vectors can be found for attacking a system.

A system's attack surface is the sum total of all possible attack vectors that malicious parties can exploit to compromise the system's security. Generally, the size of the attack surface increases as the system expands with more software code and additional hardware, computing machines, routing/switching devices, cabling, people, etc. For small systems, attack surface analyzing software tools can be used to keep track of any changes to the attack surface.

By understanding attack vectors and the attack surface, you can pick up clues that the upcoming widespread adoption of IoT will significantly increase the attack surface. In warfare, defenders have to manage all of their vulnerabilities and insecurities, whereas attackers need only one or a few vulnerabilities to focus attacks. In other words, defenders must have countermeasures for all attack vectors, but attackers only need to exploit one or few attack vectors. This makes defense a daunting task for large attack surfaces, but it provides attackers with greater freedom of action and more opportunities for attack options. Therefore, the widespread implementation of IoT presents information security professionals with a tough task.

3.2 Large-Scale DDoS Attacks

Denial of service (DoS) attacks have been a menace for the business world. These attacks prevent legitimate users of a system from accessing required information from the system. The effect of a DoS attack varies in intensity based on these factors:

- The number of users affected
- The range of its spread
- The duration of time that the system is unavailable

A DoS attack is typically launched by generating a number of unsolicited requests beyond the system's capacity to a resource, server, or service provider. Flooding the system leaves nothing available for some, if not all, of the system's legitimate users. This means that a common way to stop a DoS attack is blocking the source generating the unwelcome requests.

If multiple sources are generating requests for a DoS attack, the attack, now called a distributed denial of service (DDoS) attack, is very difficult for the defender to block due to the number of sources. When a popular service is rendered unavailable to its legitimate users for some time, the victim service can bear huge financial loss and embarrassment. For example, in 2012, a series of DDoS attacks against

US banks caused those banks' customers to have difficulty accessing online and mobile banking.[46]

Today's DDoS attacks have become very sophisticated and threatening. Attackers commonly provide DDoS attacks as a service through software tools and botnets. Software tools can automatically generate an overwhelming amount of unsolicited requests from different sources (IP addresses), while botnets control armies of compromised systems, called *zombies*, to launch large-scale DDoS attacks. The zombies taking part in the attack might not even know that they are being used.

IoT brings new opportunities for perpetrators of DDoS attacks. A larger attack surface; a greater number of entities; currently, less secure endpoints; and a more widespread area of influence all accompany IoT. Remember the following points about the nature of IoT things:

- Expected to reach, if not exceed, trillions of devices
- Always on and online
- Generally not regularly checked for security loopholes
- Typically operate with default configurations, including admin usernames and passwords

Turning IoT entities into zombies is much easier than converting desktop computers. The impact of a DDoS attack launched through such a large number of entities would be tremendous.

Already, the Mirai botnet attack, launched in the last quarter of 2016, has demonstrated the power and devastation of a DDoS attack launched using IoT devices. Mirai worked by continuously scanning for Internet-accessible IoT devices protected only by factory default or through hardcore username/passwords settings.[47] All such devices

---

[46] https://www.cio.com/article/2389721/ddos-attacks-against-us-banks-peaked-at-60-gbps.html

[47] *Symantec Internet Security Threat Report – 2017.*

were then infected with malware, converted to zombies under the control of a central server, and used for launching DDoS attacks.

3.3 Widespread Malware Attacks

Since the advent of the Internet, malware attacks have become quite common. With the passage of time, malware attacks have grown increasingly sophisticated and more difficult to detect, despite the fact that anti-malware software is used extensively. The spread of malware has become quite easy due to the rise of the hyperconnected, online lifestyle.

Eventually, new malware comes, bypasses current defenses, and quickly spreads before an associated removal kit or new virus definition can be released. Even older malware can be modified to pass through antivirus defenses using code obfuscation and polymorphism. Ultimately, this has made defense against new malware more reactive than proactive.

The problem of malware infection and its spread will likely increase in the realm of IoT. Other than the larger attack surface of IoT, IoT's huge number of entities and widespread implementation are also catalysts for this effect. Currently, IoT is being haphazardly implemented, where the race is on to quickly manufacture IoT devices and get a bigger market share. However, these devices are likely to include limited or no built-in security, with no protection at all against malware attacks. Software upgrades and security patches may be sent at a later time, but this is a colossal task. On the other hand, IoT makes spreading malware easier, due to enhanced connectivity and the larger number of entities. As IoT grows over time, this issue might worsen, unless some concrete measures are taken to stop this speedy installation of insecure devices.

3.4 Cyberterrorism

Terrorism is already a global threat, but rapid IT advancements have created even more opportunities. Smartphones, connectivity, and virtual currencies are just a few new dimensions used by terrorists. Terrorists' networks now extensively use cyberspace to fulfill their nefarious designs.

Any form of terrorism has a political or an ideological agenda or theme behind it. Moreover, the aim of all terrorism remains the spread of fear, anxiety, and terror among the masses on a large scale. Terrorism primarily differs based on the tools, means, or methods used to create and spread the mass effects. In the case of cyberterrorism, the means of creating fear and panic among the public include IT and the Internet. This use of cyber means is what differentiates cyberterrorism from other forms of terrorism.

Although IT has already changed the way we live and breathe, IoT penetrates further into daily life. Considering the deep penetration of IoT and its reach into the masses, IoT is already expected to be a strong tool into the hands of terrorists.[48]

3.5 Ransomware

With ransomware, attackers get a foothold into a target system and encrypt all or part of the system's data. The legitimate user then receives a message to pay a ransom in exchange for the decryption key. While the attacker might not actually access the target's data, the attacker does maintain a communication channel with the victim.

A recent example of a widespread ransomware attack was the Petya ransomware in the United States and Europe during the second quarter of 2017. Victims were given a message to pay a ransom of $300 in Bitcoins and send confirmation to an email address that was immediately blocked by the email service provider. The attack started from Ukraine, where government, banking, travel, and many other industries were badly affected. The attack especially caused anxiety among many victims who paid a ransom but still could not access their data.

A month or more before Petya, the WannaCry ransomware attack surfaced worldwide. Within a day, the attack affected more than

---

[48] https://link.springer.com/article/10.1007/s40309-016-0107-z

200,000 systems spread across 150 countries. This attack targeted computers running Microsoft Windows operating systems and demanded ransom in bitcoins, just like Petya ransomware.

IoT, with its huge user base spread over the globe, is likely to continuously generate colossal amounts of data. The real benefit of IoT is the ability of controlling entities to make intelligent decisions based on filtered data. If a ransomware attack renders the data unavailable for a period of time, IoT systems would be at a complete standstill, affecting and hurting the users who relied on the systems.

3.6 Privacy Threats

The explosion of information technology has also come with an explosion of privacy concerns. The Internet, hyperconnectivity, public data repositories, and using blanket permissions for various applications have all further aggravated the problem. Merchants, in the garb of relevant advertising, and cybercriminals, in the quest for financial gains, have also worked to threaten individuals' privacy in the Internet age.

Before IoT, the gadgets that could threaten or compromise user privacy were much fewer in number. Smartphones, laptops, and desktop were the primary, if not exclusive, portals to the cyber world. But the advent of IoT is seeing the implementation of smart homes and cities, with people constantly under surveillance by a host of sensors. This has made protecting user privacy from attackers an even more daunting task.

4. IoT Security Challenges

Emanating from the threat matrix are a variety of security challenges for IoT to face. The projected large number of IoT devices will lead to an enormous amount of data that needs to be stored and protected from threat agents. Additionally, IoT devices will be exposed to a significant amount of data about personal habits and peculiarities giving rise to major privacy concerns.

4.1 Security from Origin to Destination

From the point of data generation until the data has reached its destination for storage, the complete session should be protected. The session includes the data transmission and exchange of any control messages. The protection should include guards against eavesdropping, exposure, modification, tampering, destruction, and unavailability of data.

IoT end-to-end sessions are huge in number. There are too many entities. There is too much data generation. The sensors in the things are always capturing variables and creating data. The data is traveling from multiple entities to the control machine for decision-making. The filtered data is being stored somewhere, often cloud storage, for future use. The data must also flow from cloud storage to the control and to the actuators of the entities.

Imagine the number of sessions, or *pipes*, being established among entities, from entities to storage and vice versa. Securing all of these sessions all the time may seem like overkill, but guarding the sessions and data is absolutely necessary.

The challenge only starts here. IoT entities are diverse, and many have very low computing power, battery power, and memory storage. Origin-to-destination security in the pre-IoT era mainly relied on SSL/TLS encryption and IPSec protocols. However, lightweight IoT devices may not be able to run such heavy protocols or spare so many resources for those measures. Therefore, IoT end-to-end security remains a challenge requiring lightweight solutions on a wide scale.

4.2 Securing Data

Data security has been practiced for as long as data storage has been common. The challenge of data security arises from the increasing amount of data that will need to be secured in the near future.

Cisco estimates in its "Cloud Index White Paper" that by 2019, the data generated by IoT devices will touch 507.5 zettabytes (1 ZB = 10^{21} bytes or 1 sextillion byte) per year, approximately 42.3 ZB per month.[49] Additionally, the data created by IoT devices is expected to be 269 times more than the data being forwarded to data centers by edge devices and 49 times more than total data center traffic. Securing that much data is difficult to comprehend.

On the other hand, the scope of IoT means that IoT data breaches will be more threatening and devastating, compared with pre-IoT era data breaches. IoT promises to automate many processes that, if hacked or tampered, would impact public and individual safety. Pilotless planes, driverless cars, and IoT-enabled health machines are just a few examples of technologies where data breaches could be life-threatening for users.

Efficient data security mechanisms are an essential requirement for the success of IoT. These mechanisms should use minimum overhead to provide confidentiality, integrity, and availability for data.

4.3 IAM (Identity and Access Management) Controls

IAM techniques provide the proper entities with access to relevant resources within the appropriate timeframe. IAM begins with the process of authentication; entities requesting access are identified using credentials or properties. The next step is authorization; authenticated entities are given access privileges based on their roles or attributes. Closely linked to IAM is user management through some system that assigns and records user roles and rights. Attributes pertaining to users' rights are kept in a central repository accessible to the IAM system.

---

[49] http://cisco.com/c/en/us/solutions/collateral/service-provider/global-cloud-index-gci/Cloud_Index_White_Paper.html; https://blogs.cisco.com/sp/the-zettabyte-era-officially-begins-how-much-is-that

There are a few problems envisioned for IAM in an IoT environment. One obvious issue is the added complexity based on IoT's huge number of entities. The other issue is that, traditionally, IAM systems have been implemented to authenticate and authorize human beings. However, IoT is expected to rely more on physical entities than human beings, which is why security experts refer to IAM in an IoT environment as IDoT (Identity of Things). Adopting IDoT will require finding solutions capable of efficiently and correctly handling the enormous size of the environment.

4.4 Cyber Laws and Regulations

Plenty of rules and regulations govern cyber use around the world. IoT will require similar regulations, but the scope of IoT presents a significant challenge. To flourish globally, IoT implementation requires an environment similar in restrictions and freedoms worldwide. This requires the development of universal IoT-focused cyber laws, possible only by creating world bodies with power to make global IoT laws. However, the creation of these bodies and laws is immediately challenged by various national biases and interests.

4.5 Privacy

Privacy is already a major information security issue for social media, smartphones, hyperconnectivity, etc. Privacy is also, arguably, the biggest apprehension for end users regarding IoT. Because IoT devices are expected to sense personal habits and peculiarities, a significant impact is expected for individual privacy. The uphill task of recording and storing this personal information presents a colossal task for the IoT market and is expected to define the confidence, adoption, and success of IoT for end users.

Conclusion

Individuals and organizations are ready to embrace IoT. However, there are already too many apprehensions about IoT security. But this does not mean that IoT is a failure.

Apprehensions regarding IoT security are already being addressed and managed alongside its implementation. Identifying IoT security concerns now benefits the IoT environment in the future. Time allows issues to be properly identified and handled. Many international bodies are already working on IoT standardization to bring stability to the IoT development process. The instances of attacks on IoT devices may slow down, but they will not likely stop IoT adoption.

CHAPTER 4
Cloud Computing and Big Data

Introduction

IoT, due to its widespread scope, huge number of entities, and large volume of associated data, is closely related to the concepts of big data and cloud computing. IoT data fulfills all of the necessary conditions to be considered big data, and IoT relies heavily on the existing cloud services infrastructure.

The merger of big data analytics and cloud computing services with IoT means that all three share security issues. Therefore, understanding the basic concepts of big data and cloud computing is an important foundation for building a knowledge of IoT security.

The security challenges faced by enterprises in today's threat environment are greater than before due to increased globalization, enhanced connectivity, and extra automation. Analyzing these present challenges provides an indication of what security challenges can be expected in the future.

1. Characteristics of IoT Data

Data generated by the Internet of Things consists of several features:

- Huge in volume
- Constantly growing
- Stored in diverse formats (video, text, images, structured, semi-structured, unstructured, etc.)
- Analyzed in real time
- Used in decision-making

This backdrop makes it easy to understand why cloud and big data are so important to the IoT agenda.

2. IoT Data Is Big Data

Big data, as the name indicates, refers to large volumes of data. Generally, petabytes of data, stored across many machines, comprising different types/formats are classified as big data. Such data normally relies on data mining techniques to identify patterns, formulate relationships, and solve problems through data analysis. Big data can take one of three forms:

- **Structured Data.** Includes data in definite arrangements like SQL databases.
- **Unstructured Data.** Unorganized data such as text, spoken scripts, and numbers.
- **Semi-structured Data.** Not arranged in a database but still includes some tags or markers to help in its organization.

Understanding IoT data as big data can also be explained through the concept of the *3 V's*:

- **Volume.** Massive amounts of data are the defining trait of big data. In the case of IoT, these huge data volumes are generated by the various entities that make up IoT.

- **Variety.** Another characteristic of big data is the variety of data formats and types. IoT data comprises different file types; structures; and forms, including structured, semi-structured, and unstructured data.
- **Velocity.** Velocity refers to the speed of processing and analysis needed for the data. Big data, to be of real value, has to be swiftly analyzed for rendering result-oriented outcomes. The same applies to IoT data, as its real benefit can be accrued only through real-time analytics.

3. Big Data Analytics for IoT

Because IoT data is big data, its diverse nature and colossal volumes require real-time analysis to make efficient decisions and take necessary actions. The outcome of IoT data analytics should be actionable intelligence that is responsible for automated actions.

3.1 Essentials of IoT Data Analytics

Data analysis for IoT data includes the following steps.

- **Collection.** First, the data from different sources is collected. However, rather than bringing all of the generated data into the data repository, the data must be efficiently filtered. Then, the data, due to the inclusion of various makes and types from multiple sources, must be arranged and sorted.
- **Processing.** The processing step takes the data through intelligence extraction algorithms and codes. This converts the data into information that can be used to make decisions.
- **Aggregation and Visualization.** Data converted into information can be applied to one particular problem and then aggregated by putting related information together. This process, similar to correlation and fusion of information, sets the stage for intelligent decision-making.

3.2 Outcomes of Data Analytics

After analysis comes action. Possible outcomes can fall into one or more categories:[50]

- **Descriptive** (*What is happening?*) This simple type of outcome tells what is happening. For example, a speedometer displays the current speed of a vehicle.
- **Diagnostic** (*Why did it happen?*) Diagnostic outcomes should explain why some event occurred. For example, diagnostic outcomes should answer why a car is not decelerating in spite of applying brakes or what has caused a change in a room's humidity.
- **Predictive** (*What is likely to happen?*) Predictive outcomes explain the likelihood of an event's occurrence. Examples of predictive outcomes include the expected life of an instrument or the probability of a natural disaster, such as an earthquake or a flood.
- **Prescriptive** (*What should I do about it?*) Prescriptive outcomes recommend actions in case of some expected occurrence. For example, prescriptive outcomes for a smart refrigerator would be the items it would need to order if the temperature rises.

4. Security Concerns for Big Data and IoT

4.1 Privacy

One of the security concerns of big data analytics is the exposure of private or personally identifiable information.[51] Large-scale data analysis creates information with significant privacy concerns. Machine learning can make connections that might not be apparent from the original data. IoT provides even more data that can be used and analyzed this way.

---

[50] David Hanes, Patrick Grossetete, Jerome Henry, Gonzalo Salgueiro, Robert Barton. *IoT Fundamentals: Networking Technologies, Protocols, and Use Cases for the Internet of Things* (Cisco Press, 2017).

[51] http://blog.learningtree.com/five-big-data-security-challenges/

4.2 Insider threats

Large volumes and varieties of data are features of both big data and IoT. As a prerequisite for data analytics and business intelligence, all data is collected and passed through various steps. This cumbersome task requires lots of human intervention, such as administration, logging, auditing, inspecting, and verifying. Staff must also typically pass a rigorous security clearance process. However, the threat of a rogue or compromised employee cannot be ruled out. This potent threat for big data analytics becomes even bigger in an IoT environment, due to the increase in data.

Configuration Management

As vendors focus more towards the emerging requirements of organizations regarding big data and analytics, security has become a lower priority. In fact, the latest tools and configurations do little to address security challenges.

For example, NoSQL data storages have gained more popularity in recent years. However, while these storages can handle large datasets, they are also difficult to secure. Similarly, many open source tools have been developed to aid in analytics. However, these tools have also created problems for configuration management.

IoT will also see security challenges similar to those faced by big data. However, IoT is also likely to make the situation more complex by adding bigger volumes and varieties of data and by bringing even more open-source tools.

4.3 Maintenance

Handling large amounts of data requires constant maintenance of the data repository. As data volumes increase, as in the case of big data and IoT data, the need for periodic maintenance also increases.

However, such maintenance—consisting of reading logs, checking for inconsistencies, and auditing—also becomes increasingly difficult to maintain.

Big data in general and IoT data in particular, if not maintained properly, slowly and gradually become useless. Sluggish analyses, instability of fields, and security lapses are all potential costs of not maintaining data. In addition, while such security lapses start as compromised integrity, they can also lead to confidentiality or availability compromises.

5. Why IoT Needs the Cloud

Cloud computing provides organizations and individuals with processing, software, infrastructure, and storage services for use in their local IT projects and systems. A *cloud* consists of a large number of server machines dedicated to providing requested services to clients. The primary benefit of cloud services is that enterprises can concentrate on their prime business instead of IT infrastructure.

Cloud computing is especially important for IoT data in one specific way: storage. Typical IoT devices have limited computing power, light power requirements, and small storage space. To handle data storage for the huge amounts of IoT data, IoT relies on the cloud for data storage.

To fully comprehend the link between IoT and the cloud, it also helps to highlight the relevance and significance of cloud computing solutions for IoT implementation.

5.1 Cloud Service Provisioning Models and Implications for IoT

Cloud providers deliver services through a variety of models. The three standard models defined by the National Institute of Standards and Technology (NIST) are *software as a service* (SaaS), *platform as a service* (PaaS), and *infrastructure as a service* (IaaS).[52] In addition to the three standard models, there are other service models that are popular in the market including *security as a service* (SECaaS) and *mobile backend as a service* (MBaaS).

- **Software as a Service (SaaS).** In this model, the provider makes various software applications available to clients. The clients can then use the applications without installing them on their terminals. This allows for lower initial costs and a quicker and easier deployment. However, a drawback to the model is that clients also have no control over the underlying operating system and infrastructure for the applications.

  IoT endeavors to add automation and intelligent decision-making into the existing process of SaaS. Every IoT entity has to be governed by some software application, but IoT entities do not typically have the necessary internal storage to run those applications. SaaS presents an especially useful solution for the problem of hosting IoT applications.

- **Platform as a Service (PaaS).** The goal of this model is to provide clients underlying operating systems, libraries, and tools to develop and install new applications. The clients have liberty of action regarding their applications, but they cannot interfere with the underlying platform.

  Lightweight and mobile operating systems are available for small devices, but PaaS can also make IoT device manufacturing easier. When manufacturers can rely on the cloud to provide a software platform for their devices, all they need to create are hardware resources with reliable network connectivity.

---

[52] Peter Mell and Timothy Grance *The NIST Definition of Cloud Computing* (Technical report). National Institute of Standards and Technology: US Department of Commerce. doi:10.6028/NIST.SP.800-145. Special publication 800-145. September 2011.

- **Infrastructure as a Service (IaaS).** In this case, the provider only provides infrastructure: processing power, main memory, storage space, etc. The choice of software layers, including operating systems, development tools, and applications, is then left to the clients.

  IoT devices, requiring more hardware resources in terms of computing power, memory, or storage, can always rely on the cloud's infrastructural services. There is no need to overload the devices with high-end hardware and increasing power requirements.

- **Security as a Service (SECaaS).** The rising trend of outsourcing information security is known as *security as a service* (SECaaS). In this model, a service provider provides enterprises with security services, including identity and access management, malware protection, intrusion detection, and incident response management.[53]

  Many security experts are not ready to outsource their systems' security. However, the widespread deployment of IoT devices with overlooked security aspects has raised many questions about built-in security. Manufacturers believe built-in security prevents a speedy rollout of IoT. Against this backdrop, cloud security services can come to the rescue. Therefore, enterprises should implement carefully planned mechanisms for security, including incorporating cloud services where possible.

- **Mobile Backend as a Service (MBaaS).** Mobile devices have an authoritative role in the IoT environment, controlling many day-to-day processes and resources. Therefore, *mobile backend*

---

[53] A. Furfaro, A. Garro, A. Tundis, "Towards Security as a Service (SecaaS): On the modeling of Security Services for Cloud Computing". *2014 International Carnahan Conference on Security Technology (ICCST)*: 1–6. doi:10.1109/CCST.2014.6986995. October 1, 2014.

as a service (MBaaS) allows mobile application developers to link their apps with the cloud for application programming interfaces and software development kits.[54] Any cloud services that facilitate application development or hosting can expedite and assist in mobile device supremacy.

5.2 Cloud Deployment Models and Their Implications for IoT

In addition to providing various services to clients, cloud deployment is also related to IoT requirements, through use of the following models:

- **Private Cloud.** In this deployment model, a single organization utilizes the cloud for its computing, storage, or infrastructural needs. The cloud may be established onsite or off-premises, managed either by the organization itself or by a third party. This arrangement requires a lot of resources and effort from the organization on a regular basis. While a private cloud may not provide most of the benefits of cloud computing, some organizations still rely on it due to their sensitivity toward security.

  Private cloud deployment does not seem like a match for the IoT environment because IoT requires openness, connectivity, and sharing as key features, unlike private cloud deployment. Secluded systems are also not typically looking for the benefits of IoT.

- **Public Cloud.** Public clouds are deployed for widespread use through the Internet. Other than the difference in users, there is hardly any difference between public and private clouds as far as technical implementation is concerned. Organizations can use these services under different payment packages, including free packages. However, a drawback with public cloud deployment is that it is less secure than the private cloud deployment model.

---

[54] Alex Williams "Kii Cloud Opens Doors For Mobile Developer Platform With 25 Million End Users," *TechCrunch*. October 11, 2012. Retrieved October 16, 2012.

From an IoT perspective, public cloud deployment offers more benefits than private cloud deployment. Because IoT promotes sharing of resources, enhanced network connectivity, and active engagement, it can use public cloud to its advantage. Public cloud can offer economical computing resources, storage space, and customized platforms, which will benefit the Internet of Things.

- **Hybrid Cloud.** As the name indicates, hybrid deployment is a combination of public and private cloud deployment models, with distinct boundaries for public and private areas. This model offers flexibility for organizations desiring to utilize both public and private services. For example, an organization may host services considered sensitive on a private cloud application but interface it with a business intelligence application offered on a public cloud as a software service.[55]

Hybrid deployment models can be used in some IoT instances where sensitivity of data or applications is important, but the scope of project needs to form part of the IoT umbrella. For example, in a smart city project, as shown in fig. 4.6, administrators may want to put some classified data onto a private cloud but also make it accessible to a public cloud, through secure interfaces.

6. Security Concerns for Cloud Computing and IoT

6.1 Provider and Client Perspectives

Security issues pertaining to cloud computing are equally relevant for the future of IoT. There are two broad categories of cloud security: aspects relevant to cloud service providers and those related to the customers.

Cloud service providers bear the responsibility of security related to their services. For example, in the case of storage provision, it is the

---

[55] "Business Intelligence Takes to Cloud for Small Businesses," CIO.com. June 4, 2014.

responsibility of the provider to ensure that its clients' data is safe and secure.

However, clients in cloud computing scenarios also have their own security responsibilities. Ensuring proper authentication and authorization and prohibiting infection of the cloud with malicious codes or files are just some examples of responsibilities for cloud computing clients.

6.2 Identity and Access Management

Cloud data, especially in the case of public cloud models, is prone to public attacks through the Internet. When sharing resources from a public cloud, clients must rely on *identity and access management* (IAM) systems, which are systems which manage electronic and digital identities. Cloud providers normally incorporate clients' IAM systems into their own.

However, IoT entities, when used with the cloud, have the potential to overwhelm IAM systems and create new, exploitable vulnerabilities that bypass the IAM system. Additionally, in spite of elaborate IAM mechanisms, the data may remain vulnerable due to poor configuration settings or clients' carelessness or complacency. Even a single unprotected device can jeopardize an IAM system if the device's login credentials are not kept safe. Already, IoT devices operating with factory default settings are too common.

6.3 Cloud Physical Security

The cloud's physical security carries significant importance in the IoT environment. The cloud is likely to be the location for most IoT data, many IoT applications, and in some cases, the IoT system's platform. In the future world of IoT, weak physical security for the cloud may allow forces in warlike situations to easily target public clouds and cripple IoT systems.

6.4 Privacy and Trust Concerns

Recent years have seen increased evidence of the cloud being misused to access people's personal information. Events, such as celebrity photo hack scandals, have already demonstrated the typically loose privacy controls of cloud computing. And yet, IoT data will include more personal information, such as data from many devices that are, or will be, installed inside homes.

Governments have admitted to collecting information from the cloud to gather intelligence for security reasons. This has rendered cloud computing, especially located in the United States, untrustworthy for many people. These concerns about privacy and lack of trust may cause problems for the nexus of IoT and cloud computing before it has a chance to take off.

Conclusion

Big data analytics seems to be the right answer to handle the volume, variety, and velocity of IoT data. Therefore, any further progress achieved in the area of big data analytics will also allow IoT data analytics to make better decisions and gain additional intelligence and agility.

Similarly, cloud computing, already developed and ready to support the IoT challenge, meets IoT needs for swift rollout and implementation of interconnected, lightweight entities.

Technologies like big data analytics and cloud computing are critical for facilitating IoT implementation and speeding up widespread rollout. However, these technologies might also augment the security woes of IoT with their own vulnerabilities. Fortunately, the individual safeguards applied to big data and cloud computing will assist in making the IoT environment more secure. However, the combination of IoT, big data analytics, and cloud computing may also create new, additional attack vectors.

CHAPTER 5

IoT Networks and Data Communications

Introduction

IoT networking is an important part of the IoT landscape. The existing global network (the Internet) offers much to IoT, but the network still needs preparation to be ready for the IoT challenge.

Understanding IoT networking and data communication requires learning about the specific networking challenges and associated security risks of IoT, compared with the existing network infrastructure.

By visualizing IoT network requirements from the perspective of a network expert, conclusions can be drawn about IoT networking needs and special mechanisms needed to attain machine-to-machine communication for IoT sensors and actuators. *Wireless sensor and actuator networks* (WSANs)[56] are the major networking need of IoT. WSANs ensure data communication and exchange among entities and with the global network.

IoT networks in general and WSANs in particular have their own information security aspects, which includes vulnerabilities and

---

[56] A group of sensors and actuators wirelessly linked and working together.

threats visible to attackers. Popular WSAN technology standards offer some useful security features, but only a few of them are being fully utilized by manufacturers today.

1. IoT Networking and Data Communication Needs

The Internet is an already existing, elaborate network that hosts the World Wide Web and many other services. However, that may not be enough for IoT. Due to the widespread scope involved in IoT, the large amounts of data, and other requirements, certain additions and modifications are required to make the Internet compatible with IoT implementation.

1.1 Widespread Scope

IoT has a much bigger scope than the pre-IoT Internet. While the pre-IoT Internet includes desktop machines, laptops, tablets, smartphones, and a few other gadgets, IoT endeavors to bring as many entities as possible onto the global network. Gartner expects the number of entities in IoT to reach 20.4 billion by 2020.[57] The present network size must increase significantly to accommodate all IoT entities.

However, today's current Internet protocols, like IPv4, are unable to handle the number of IP addresses that will be required for IoT. Mechanisms will need to be devised to manage IP addresses, access network bandwidth requirements, handle congestion, detect and correct errors, and control flow in this greatly expanded network.

1.2 Wireless Security

IoT's widened network size and scope also leads to bigger security challenges. In many cases, additional network infrastructure will be provided by adding wireless networks. However, wireless networks face greater security threats than wired networks. Therefore, better wireless network security is a need for IoT.

---

[57] http://www.gartner.com/newsroom/id/3598917

1.3 Data Communications and Bandwidth Requirements

IoT devices are constantly communicating. Most IoT entities use built-in sensors to constantly monitor their environments for relevant variables and transmit the collected data to control entities for further processing and analysis. The resulting control signals then travel from control entities to the relevant devices for action by the actuators.

Additionally, most IoT entities are so lightweight that they have little storage space. Therefore, most data storage must take place in cloud storage. This means that a large amount of data traffic is going from entities to the cloud and vice versa.

These data exchange requirements make IoT data communication and bandwidth requirements critical for any proposed IoT network architectures.

1.4 Unrestrained Networks

The interconnecting network devices of IoT are typically so lightweight that they should have long battery lives. However, this also means the devices should need little computing power and memory. These constraints restrict network bandwidth to a bare minimum.

The IoT environment's peculiarities demand constrained networking technologies and techniques. This need is especially clear for lightweight, edge devices[58] extended over long distances.

1.5 Large Volumes of Data

IoT requires large volumes of data for analysis and efficient decision-making. Also, the data processing cycle requires that the data is filtered, collated, sifted, and integrated before it can be properly used. These

---

[58] Devices that process data closer to where the data is produced rather than in data centers or clouds.

actions must be performed at various stages of transmission through the IoT network to avoid creating bottlenecks.

1.6 Legacy Network Devices

Because of the Internet, a lot of network infrastructure already exists to support IoT implementation, rollout, and hosting. Over time, network devices specific to the peculiar needs of IoT devices will emerge, along with new protocols and standards. Additionally, existing network entities and protocols will likely be amalgamated according to IoT standards. Legacy devices and protocols may require a few modifications and upgrades, but generally, they should be able to be used in the IoT landscape. This would speed up IoT implementation faster than if legacy devices and protocols needed to be dismantled and replaced.

1.7 Real-Time Data Analytics

The need for real-time analysis of IoT data has repercussions for IoT networking. Data analysis engines should be close to where the data is generated in order to avoid unnecessarily long data transmission. Therefore, IoT networking infrastructure should facilitate sufficient processing power and storage placement close to the edge devices.

2. How IoT Networking Works

Understanding IoT networking requires considering what entities need to be networked. Typical IoT networks include the following:

- **IoT Devices/Things.** IoT devices should be able to access, store, send, and receive data whenever necessary. This usually means that the data they generate might have to be kept at a central repository.

  But IoT is not a centralized system; it is a distributed system. The entities have specific data exchange and bandwidth requirements. Since the devices are mostly lightweight, functions involving data, applications, or even processing, may be outsourced to a cloud.

- **Localized Networks of Entities.** Local networks connect entities operating in environments with similar scopes or areas of influence, for speedy communication. These networks must be highly agile, likely ad hoc, and mostly wireless, with constraints. They may also have to handle proprietary devices, protocols, standards, etc.

- **The Internet.** Local IoT networks need interoperability with the Internet to make the individual systems part of a single global network. They need to share information to create shared awareness.

  Because the language of the Internet is the Internet Protocol (IP), local IoT networks may require some translation services for converting IP to proprietary, local network protocols and vice versa.

- **Backend Services.** IoT networks must also cater to backend services. Examples include data storage, clouds, IAM systems, etc.

3. WSAN—The Local Network of Entities

In IoT systems, sensors and actuators are to be connected together to form a network called a wireless sensor and actuator network (WSAN). This network forwards data through lightweight nodes and uses special-purpose nodes on its edges to interface between the local network and the Internet.

WSANs operate in environments with one or more of the following properties:

- **Wireless Communications.** Most of the IoT devices, sensors, and actuators are manufactured with wireless networking capability.
- **Mobility.** Mobility is important for WSAN protocols, especially since the nodes and clients are typically lightweight devices with limited processing power and storage.
- **Flexibility.** Nodes and clients change their locations frequently, due to the ad hoc nature of the IoT landscape; therefore, different topologies[59] need to be considered.

3.1 Variables in WSAN Technologies

WSAN technologies can be differentiated from each other by several variables.

- **Coverage Area.** WSAN technologies offer different ranges of communication around WSAN nodes. Additionally, choosing outdoor or indoor deployment impacts WSAN technology choices. Table 5.1 depicts area coverage ranges of several available technologies.

	Coverage Area	WSAN Technologies
1.	Short Range (<10 meters)	IEEE 802.15.1 Bluetooth IEEE 802.15.7 VLC
2.	Medium Range (10-100 meters)	IEEE 802.11 Wi-Fi IEEE 802.15.4 802.15.4g WPAN IEEE 802.3 Ethernet IEEE 1901.2 Narrow Band PLC
3.	Long Range (> mile)	Cellular 2G, 3G, 4G Outdoor IEEE 802.11 Wi-Fi Low-Power Wide-Area (LPWA) technologies

Table 5.1. Approximate coverage areas of popular WSAN technologies

---

[59] The arrangement of the elements of a network.

- **Frequency Range.** Usable frequency bands for wireless technologies are governed by different regulations in different countries. Long-range wireless communication technologies can be employed, but only after necessary licensing. However, for short-range communication, some unlicensed bands also exist.
- **Power Requirements of WSAN Nodes.** The power arrangement of nodes is important for IoT, given the billions of entities expected. The question of whether the nodes require wired power or batteries makes a huge impact on WSAN technology choices. Additionally, if the WSAN nodes are battery-powered, it is worth considering the duration the batteries can sustain without recharging or replacement.
- **Dominant Topologies.** Three main topologies are commonly employed by WSANs for IoT access networks: star, mesh, and peer-to-peer.
  - *Star topology.* A star-like arrangement is formed by a central node facilitating communication with edge points.
  - *Mesh topology.* Repeater nodes handle low power while transmitting at longer distances.
  - *Peer-to-peer topology.* Any node can communicate with any other node in range. Therefore, all the nodes in peer-to-peer are operated with full sets of functions.
- **Constrained Nodes.** IoT access networks include quite a few nodes on lightweight devices with limited resources. Such nodes are called *constrained nodes*. These constrained nodes, unlike computers and smartphones, possess limited processing power, main memory, and storage capacity.

3.2 IoT Protocols and Standards

Because various IoT protocols implement functionalities at different networking layers, network implementation requires a combination of protocols. Wi-Fi, Bluetooth, Zigbee, Z-wave, and LoRaWAN are a few of the popular protocols, standards, and technologies that operate at the data link layer, whereas 6LowPAN and Thread protocols operate at the network layer.[60]

- **Bluetooth**. This old protocol, used for short-range data communications, has been in use since 1994, operating in the 2.4 to 2.485 GHz ISM band. It is commonly used for building *personal area networks* (PANs).[61] A special interest group of telecommunications companies oversees the development of the Bluetooth standard.

  Bluetooth, in the IoT environment, is being utilized in wearable IoT devices. *Bluetooth low-energy* (BLE), also called *Bluetooth smart*, modified for low power consumption, is widely used in IoT applications. The added advantage of Bluetooth smart is that it can allow sensors to interact directly with IP networks and the Internet.

- **Zigbee.** Zigbee is another popular IoT protocol, designed for creating PANs of lightweight devices. Zigbee is based on the IEEE802.15.4 industry standard, operates at 2.4 GHz, and is preferably employed for coverage areas within 100 meters. Zigbee supports star, mesh, and peer-to-peer topologies.

  Every Zigbee network has a coordinator node tasked with network maintenance. Zigbee follows the physical and MAC layer definitions of IEEE802.15.4 for low-rate wireless PANs. Network nodes operating on Zigbee can run on batteries for years. Zigbee also supports secure communication, which is a big plus in the IoT environment.

- **Z-Wave.** Z-wave is a highly optimized protocol for limited latency and reliable communication, with data rates as high as

---

[60] *See* chapter 2, "IoT Architecture and Design," for a review of the different IoT layers.
[61] A computer network that allows for communication between devices near a person (e.g., smartphones, tablets, and computers).

100 kbps. Its primary application is in home-automation items, such as refrigerators, air conditioners, and lamps. Z-wave uses the sub-1 GHz band; therefore, it does not interfere with technologies like Wi-Fi, Bluetooth, and Zigbee which operate in the 2.4 GHz range. Z-wave can provide interoperability between devices built by manufacturers who are part of the Z-wave alliance. Z-wave devices can communicate with each other in a mesh topology, allowing messages to be sent to destination devices not in range, since the message can be relayed through another device.

- **Wi-Fi.** Wi-Fi is a widely used standard for home, office, and academic institution short-range networking. It is IP-based and is easily merged into the global network through simple routing techniques. It can also reliably handle fast data exchange rates in tens of mbps.

  However, legacy Wi-Fi power consumption needs typically created difficulties for lightweight IoT applications and devices. Therefore, two new Wi-Fi standards have emerged to cater for IoT needs: 802.11ah (*Wi-Fi HaLow*) and 802.11ax (*High-Efficiency Wireless, or HEW*).

  Wi-Fi HaLow surfaced in the last quarter of 2016, particularly addressing the range and power issues of the earlier Wi-Fi standard. It operates in the 900 MHz range and uses defined phases of *wake* and *doze* to conserve power. The coverage area is also extended by a station-grouping feature.

  HEW is a further enhancement of Wi-Fi HaLow, making use of earlier modifications and augmenting it with a few more. These new standards may still not be the best choice for IoT, but the huge base of already-installed Wi-Fi devices, if upgraded, could give a boost to IoT infrastructure development.

- **Cellular.** Existing cellular communication technologies like GSM, 3G, and 4G can be used for IoT networking. Although using cellular networks as IoT hosts has obvious drawbacks, like high power consumption, limited coverage area, and high costs, existing cellular communication setups can be handy for limited, long-haul IoT traffic.

- **Near Field Communication (NFC) Technology.** NFC protocols facilitate data exchange between two electronic devices within 4 cm of each other. NFC is already used in contactless payments through credit cards, e-ticketing cards, and smartphones. NFC uses a frequency range of 13.56 MHz for contactless air interface. Data transfer rates of 106 to 424 kbps can be achieved through NFC.

- **Sigfox.** Sigfox is designed for machine-to-machine communications with a coverage area somewhere between Wi-Fi and cellular. It supports low-powered nodes with limited data exchange rates, approximately in the range of 10 to 1000 bps. Its typical standby time for a node is almost twenty years for a 2.5 Ah battery. Sigfox is already seeing widespread use in IoT networks in European countries.

- **LoRaWAN.** This protocol is used by wide area networks (WANs)[62] operating at the MAC layer. It primarily facilitates long-range wireless communications between low-powered IoT WSANs and the Internet. It has capacity for a huge number of nodes, into the millions. The typical rate of data exchange ranges from 0.3 to 50 kbps.

- **6LowPAN.** The *IPv6 Low-Power Wireless Personal Area Network* protocol, nicknamed *6LowPAN*, is an IP based protocol designed

---

[62] A network that extends over a wide geographic area usually to connect multiple computers.

to ensure that low-powered devices could use the IP protocol and be part of IoT.[63]

Header compression and encapsulation techniques employed in 6LowPAN allow for packet exchange between IEEE802.15.4-based networks. Unlike Zigbee and Bluetooth, 6LoWPAN is a network protocol. The way 6LowPAN uses frequency and physical layer technology allows it to be employed across various different communication platforms, like Ethernet, IEEE802.15.4, Wi-Fi, and sub-1GHz band.

- **Thread.** This is another IPv6 based protocol, designed on 6LowPAN, with a goal of facilitating home networks. It surfaced in 2014, by the initiative of a research group called Thread, as a royalty-free protocol. It utilizes various standards like IEEE802.15.4, IPv6, and 6LowPAN. Thread is capable of handling a mesh network of up to 250 nodes. It also provides encryption and authentication mechanisms.

4. Securing IoT Networks

IoT network architecture, protocols, standards, and technologies are evolving with the passage of time. As a result, IoT network security must also evolve to meet new challenges.

IoT network security discussion is primarily concerned with the security aspects of WSANs because they are the part of IoT network security most different from legacy network security. Unfortunately, WSAN security aspects are typically given the lowest priority upon implementation. IoT is rolling out urgently, with large amounts of devices being added daily into the IoT landscape. But manufacturers are not paying enough attention to the security aspects of the implementation. If they are not

---

[63] Zach Shelby and Carsten Bormann, "6LoWPAN: The wireless embedded Internet - Part 1: Why 6LoWPAN?"*EE Times*, May 23, 2011.

implemented carefully, security features offered in WSAN technologies and protocols are rendered useless. Haphazard deployment with an urgency mindset has made WSAN implementation a complex affair susceptible to security lapses and loopholes.

IoT's widespread scope means that WSAN nodes are likely to be installed anywhere and connected wirelessly. However, these locations may be accessible by malicious actors, especially since wireless communication is susceptible to attacks spread through omnidirectional coverage, as with IoT. Popular attacks on wireless communications include interruption, eavesdropping, modification, and masquerading.

4.1 Common WSAN Attacks

- **Wormhole Attack.** In this form of attack on WSANs, the attacker establishes a malicious node as part of the network. The attacker then uses the malicious node to receive legitimate messages (known as *interception* or *eavesdropping*) and can pass them to other nodes after modification. Alternatively, instead of establishing a new node, the attacker may compromise an existing node to perpetrate the attack.

- **Side-Channel Attack on WSAN Nodes.** Side-channel attacks capture leakage information, such as power traces, heat/photonic emissions, and timing information, from devices and correlate that information with data processing to determine cryptographic keys. This is normally a difficult attack because the device access required may be difficult for an adversary to obtain. However, the IoT scenario, with devices installed in billions, provides significantly more opportunities for access by a determined attacker.

- **Spoofing Attack.** Attackers, after imitating one legitimate entity, can use that entity's access to spread infections through the network. IP spoofing, MAC spoofing, and message spoofing are different examples. For example, IP spoofing can be used by attackers to imitate the IP address of a legitimate device in order to send malicious traffic to others as if coming from the legitimate entity.

- **Distributed Denial of Service (DDoS) Attack.** In an IoT scenario, DDoS attacks can be devastating for not only WSANs but for the global network. DDoS attacks use infected devices to overwhelm network devices with unsolicited requests beyond their handling capacity, making the devices unavailable to legitimate users. Insecure WSANs have plenty of devices that attackers can infect, control, and use to launch DDoS attacks.

- **Illegal Network Access.** Illegal network access tends to be easier to obtain in the case of WSANs, since the devices are often not properly configured or hardened. Factory-default login credentials left on even one sensor or device can jeopardize the security of an entire WSAN. Then, once the access has been obtained, it can lead to any other form of attack.

- **Exploitation of Insecure WSAN Protocols.** Several WSAN protocols may no longer be considered secure due to known vulnerabilities. However, when these protocols are still used, they provide easy access to attackers trying to penetrate into the network. Examples of these protocols include the following:[64]
  o Modbus protocol suffers from authentication issues.
  o Distributed Network Protocol (DNP3) has a few insecure versions.
  o Inter-control Center Communications Protocol (ICCP) suffers from authentication issues and encryption enabled by default.
  o OLE for Process Control (OPC) relies on the RPC (remote procedure call) protocol, which itself has many vulnerabilities.

---

[64] David Hanes, Patrick Grossetete, Jerome Henry, Gonzalo Salgueiro, Robert Barton, *IoT Fundamentals: Networking Technologies, Protocols, and Use Cases for the Internet of Things* (Cisco Press, 2017).

4.2 WSAN Security Configurations

Security configuration options for WSAN technologies, as illustrated in table 5.2, can be implemented during deployment. However, it is not enough just to implement security configurations; the security options must also be used.

	Standard	Security provisions
1.	IEEE 802.15.4	AES-128
		Data validation through message integrity code (MIC)
2.	IEEE 802.15.4g and 802.15.4e	AES-128
		Auxiliary Security Header Field
		Secure acknowledgment
		Secure beacon field
3.	IEEE 1901.2a	AES-128
		Key Management
4.	IEEE 802.11ah	No addition to basic IEEE 802.11
5.	LoRaWAN	Endpoints must implement two layers of security
		AES-128
		Network session key ensures data integrity through MIC
		VPN and IPSec support
		Authentication mechanism

Table 5.2. Security provisions in popular WSAN standards

Conclusion

IoT networking and data communications is a vast topic that begins with understanding IoT connectivity needs and how they are different from pre-IoT era Internet requirements. In IoT, the main entities are not computers, laptops, or smartphones; they are sensors and actuators. This is the era of machine-to-machine communication, both locally and with the global network. IoT devices are not equipped to spend many resources on computing, data storage, and battery power; the network processing has to be extremely light.

IoT devices are not in the thousands; rather, they are in the billions.[65] Also, their topology might change on the fly, so there is an element of ad hocism. All these peculiarities must be addressed in a machine-to-machine IoT network.

However, IoT networking also comes with its own information security needs. WSANs are being deployed every day, with very enthusiastic timelines. Manufacturers are constantly bringing new IoT devices into the market. There is a race to stay ahead regarding IoT, but in the process, security controls and standard protocols are often ignored. These controls must be offered, tested, and evolved for standard IoT internetworking.

Networking provides the major infrastructure for the IoT world. Its standardization, smooth implementation, and secure operation are essential for IoT success.

---

[65] https://safeatlast.co/blog/iot-statistics/

CHAPTER 6

Cryptographic Provisions for IoT

Introduction

Cryptography, the study and practice of secure communications techniques, is expected to be used in various information security services and functions. Therefore, it cannot be left out of any discussion related to information security. Major cryptographic primitives, the basic building blocks of cryptography, will be needed to implement IoT security services.

Various IoT and WSAN protocols, technologies, and standards provide options for using cryptography to provide information security features. However, while most IoT protocols have built-in cryptographic provisions, their implementation is typically left to the user's discretion. If users don't take the initiative to properly implement these provisions, then there is a strong risk that their communications will be compromised.

1. Cryptography's Essential Role in Information Security

Cryptography uses secret writing for secure communication between parties. The sender encrypts a clear message, called *plain text*, before transmission, using some cryptosystem. The encrypted message, called *cipher text*, is then transmitted by some means to the intended recipients. The receiver decrypts the cipher text, using the same cryptosystem that was used for encryption, to obtain the plain text. This means that during transmission, the cipher text cannot be understood by malicious parties even if it is intercepted.

Attackers aim to find the key or some other loophole in cipher implementation. *Brute force attacks*, which are attempts to find a decryption key by checking all possible keys, are often computationally infeasible. Therefore, *cryptanalysis*, the study of alternative methods of breaking ciphers is important. *Cryptology* is the study of both cryptography and cryptanalysis.

Security services and functions are often implemented through cryptographic algorithms, usually built according to well-known mechanisms called *cryptographic primitives*. Cryptographic primitives are the basic building blocks of a cryptographic security protocol. These primitives are especially useful in providing security services for IoT.

1.1 Confidentiality

Confidentiality means keeping information undisclosed to unauthorized parties. Only authorized users should be able to access confidential information.

In the IoT environment, entities continuously communicate through WSANs. However, such wireless communication is highly susceptible to interception. For example, IoT entities installed in smart homes would send large volumes of data, containing large amounts of personal information, to outside service providers. Exposure of such data in transit, due to lack of confidentiality controls, would mean loss of privacy and would make IoT untrustworthy. Therefore, WSAN protocols must ensure confidentiality of the data traveling on the network.

1.2 Integrity

Cryptography provides integrity by ensuring that the contents of messages are not tampered with or modified during transmission. In IoT, WSAN protocols need to provide integrity in communications.

The huge number of entities exchanging data in WSANs increases the probability of *man-in-the-middle* (MITM) attacks. MITM attacks occur when an attacker secretly intercepts communications between two or more parties to eavesdrop or alter the conversation. MITM attacks can devastatingly impact complete IoT systems because intercepted data can be modified to cause incorrect actions by the actuators. For example, if the security alarm of smart city is switched on due to a modified control signal, the actuators installed around the city might generate a set of panic actions.

1.3 Data Origin Authentication

Data origin authentication is the assurance that a received message is coming from an authentic source. In many cases, data origin authentication also confirms the integrity of the message.

Data origin authentication is especially important for IoT due to threats, such as spoofing, where attackers masquerade as legitimate entities. Because of the potential harms of these types of attacks, WSANs should use cryptography to achieve data origin authentication.

1.4 Non-Repudiation

Non-repudiation means that the sender of a message cannot deny creation of the message.

The pre-IoT era has seen non-repudiation primarily used for e-commerce. In the IoT environment, non-repudiation will be a basic requirement for gadgets to automatically order items, run supply chains, book appointments, etc. People denying that they authorized automated transactions from accounts or entities under their use would cause problems for automated transactions. Therefore, non-repudiation services are vital for IoT to build trust in the authentication of entities and the validity of IoT processes.

2. Cryptographic Primitives and Their Application in IoT

The security services cryptography makes available are attained by using basic cryptographic primitives. Once these primitives and the security services they provide are properly understood, they can be applied to the IoT environment.

2.1 Primary Cryptographic Primitives

- **Secret Key Cryptography.** *Secret key cryptography*, also known as *symmetric encryption*, has the sender and receiver possess the same key before sending any messages. The sender encrypts the message with the key and sends it to the receiver. At its end, the receiver decrypts the message with its copy of the key. Secret key cryptography is implemented into broad categories of block ciphers and stream ciphers.

    o **Block Ciphers.** *Block ciphers* break plain text into equal-sized blocks and then encrypt the blocks one after another. On the receiving end, the encrypted blocks are then decrypted sequentially to obtain the plain text. *Advanced Encryption Standard (AES)* and *Data Encryption Standard (DES)* are two examples of block ciphers.

    AES was chosen by the National Institute of Standards and Technology (NIST) through an open and transparent competition in 2000.[66] AES can be implemented with 128-bit, 192-bit, and 256-bit key sizes. Bigger key length offers more security but also requires more overhead, in terms of computing power and memory. Complete documentation of AES can be found at the NIST website.[67]

The trouble with block ciphers is that if they are provided with the same plain text and secret key, they will always create the same output cipher text. This situation is not acceptable for security purposes because it is too predictable. Therefore, block ciphers must be implemented in a way that avoids predictability. Several modes of implementation have been devised; popular ones include Cipher Block Chaining (CBC), Cipher Feedback (CFB), Output Feedback (OFB), and Counter (CTR).

o **Stream Ciphers.** *Stream ciphers* generate a continuous key stream. The plain text is used with the key stream to generate cipher text that is transmitted. The receiver has a mechanism that generates the same key stream and uses it with the cipher text to obtain the plain text. Synchronization between the key streams generated at both ends is essential.

There are two kinds of stream ciphers. *Self-synchronizing* stream ciphers, also known as *asynchronous* stream ciphers, include key stream generation as a function of previous cipher text bits. *Synchronous* stream ciphers use streams that are independent of cipher text bits.

• **Public Key Cryptography.** *Public key cryptography* allows secure communication over insecure channels without

---

[66] Commerce Department Announces Winner of Global Information Security Competition. NIST.GOV (October 12, 1997), *available at* https://www.nist.gov/news-events/news/2000/10/commerce-department-announces-winner-global-information-security.
[67] http://csrc.nist.gov/publications/fips/fips197/fips-197.pdf

pre-sharing secret keys. Every communicating party has an associated public and private key pair. Messages encrypted with one of the pairs of keys can be decrypted only with the other key of the pair. Private keys of the parties are known only to the parties themselves. Public keys of all parties are available in a central repository accessible by any communicating party that is part of the system.

This means that when a party sends a message encrypted with the receiver's public key, it can only be decrypted by the receiver itself through its private key. This ensures confidentiality of the message. Also, when a message is encrypted with a private key, any receiver decrypting it with the sender's public key can be sure of the message's origin, since senders cannot deny sending messages encrypted with their private keys.

- **Cryptographic Hash.** *Cryptographic hash* uses one-way functions to encrypt messages into a contracted fixed-length value called a *message digest* or a *hash*. No keys are used. Hash functions have several characteristics. *Pre-image resistance* requires hash functions to be irreversible, so that a message cannot be obtained from a hash. *Second pre-image resistance* means that even with a message and its hash, another message will not create the same hash. Finally, *collision resistance*, also known as *collision-free hash*, means that no two messages should lead to the same hash.

- **Message Authentication Code (MAC).**[68] *Message authentication code (MAC)* creates a cryptographic checksum of a message using a pre-shared secret key and appends it to the message before transmission. Then, on the receiving side, the message can be checked for integrity by verifying the appended MAC through the same calculations used to create the MAC with the pre-shared key. The receiver is also sure of data origin authenticity

---

[68] Figure from https://commons.wikimedia.org

because no one else can generate that MAC against the received message without possessing the pre-shared key. Including a sequence number in the message can provide added security.

- **Digital Signatures.**[69] MACs and hashes do not address the issue of non-repudiation. For example, an online order, even if made through a secure communication method, might still be denied by the alleged purchaser. The alleged purchaser might claim that the order was generated by the merchant, who also possesses the secret, pre-shared key.

  However, a digital signature effectively achieves non-repudiation. A receiver can be sure that a message is from the signer, and the signer cannot claim that receiver has created the message, because the signature is not shared between them. The receiver can then take actions based on the message without fear of the sender denying having sent the message.

2.2 Using Cryptographic Primitives for IoT Security Services

Cryptographic primitives can be applied individually or in combination to achieve various security services. They can be used to achieve confidentiality, integrity, authenticity, and non-repudiation:

- **Confidentiality (Encryption).** Confidentiality can be achieved through either secret key or public key encryption. Secret key encryption is normally preferred for long sessions. Keys can be pre-shared through public key encryption.

  WSAN protocols should use encryption for data exchange. For example, entities should be able to establish a secure tunnel through public key infrastructure and then transfer data in an end-to-end tunnel.

---

[69] Figure from https://commons.wikimedia.org

- **Integrity and Authentication (MAC or Digital Signature).** Integrity of data in transit can be ensured using MAC. Communicating parties can pre-share a secret key through public key cryptography, and then they can send and receive data while appending and verifying a MAC along with each transmission. This ensures that the data on the move would be safe from tampering and modification. If the receiving party can verify the MAC, that also implies authenticity of the party sending the message.

  Data integrity can also be also be ensured through digital signatures based on public key cryptography. Digital signatures guarantee data origin authenticity, which, logically, ensures the integrity of data in transit as well.

  IoT needs an authority for issuing public and private keys or assigning certificates. Implementing MAC or digital signature primitives into adopted WSAN protocols can ensure the integrity of data traveling among the entities and the authentication of senders.

- **Non-Repudiation (Digital Signature).** Digital signature is the only cryptographic primitive that can achieve the security service of non-repudiation. The sender has to generate the signature using its own private key, inaccessible to anyone else. The receiver can verify the signature by using the sender's public key.

  The IoT environment, with its huge number of devices, requires a strong need for not only authentication but also non-repudiation for IoT transactions. Public key infrastructure and IoT protocols can provide support for digital signature implementation.

2.3 Cryptography Implementation Example: TLS[70]

Transport Layer Security (TLS) protocol is a relevant example of how cryptographic primitives are employed within a protocol to provide security services.

TLS relies on an algorithm called RSA, which is based on public key cryptography, for pre-sharing keys and digital certificates. RSA also uses the SHA256 hashing algorithm to provide digital signatures.

AES-128, based on secret key cryptography, is used in TLS for encryption to achieve end-to-end confidentiality. This block cipher is implemented using Galois Counter Mode (GCM) encryption, which also provides MACs for TLS chunks.

3. Cryptographic Provisions in IoT Protocols[71]

Many popular IoT protocols provide for cryptographic controls. However, the implementation of these controls varies based on the protocol's configuration settings.

- **LoRaWAN** uses AES-128 encryption for confidentiality. Data integrity is provided by using network session keys at endpoints to check data messages' message integrity codes (MICs). LoRaWAN can also provide authentication support through virtual private network (VPN) implementation and IPSec tunnels.
- **Zigbee** is based on IEEE 802.15.4, which supports AES-128 for both data confidentiality and integrity through encryption/ decryption and MAC, respectively.[72] However, Zigbee can

---

[70] Brian Russell and Drew Van, "Practical Internet of Things Security," published by Packt Publishing, 2016.

[71] For a review of these different protocols, see chapter 5, "IoT Networks and Data Communications."

[72] http://www.libelium.com/security-802-15-4-zigbee/

also be used without any of the security features. Zigbee also provides preinstalled master keys from vendors for secure key exchange, as well as link keys and network keys at each node.

- **Bluetooth-LE**, as per Bluetooth Core specifications, provides cryptographic controls like pairing, end-to-end encryption, authentication, and data integrity. Pairing nodes can share keys, and devices can be authenticated for possession of trusted keys.
- **IEEE 802.15.4g and 802.15.4e** have the same cryptographic controls options as IEEE 802.15.4 2006 specifications, with primary reliance on AES-128. They have dedicated headers for security and MIC in their MAC sub-layer frames, and they rely on key management protocol (KMP) for key management.
- **IEEE 1901.2a** also offers AES-128 encryption and authentication, and it supports KMP for key management.

Conclusion

Cryptographic provisions play an important role in securing the IoT environment. Information security professionals need to understand the essentials of cryptographic controls in the complex atmosphere of IoT. Trying to secure IoT without employing cryptographic algorithms and principles would be daunting.

Almost all IoT protocols and standards can use cryptography to provide confidentiality, data integrity, data origin authenticity, and non-repudiation services. However, these protocols and standards tend to make cryptography optional, meaning it can be bypassed or ignored. Because haphazard and speedy deployment are common in the race to manufacture more IoT devices, it is not astonishing to see disabled cryptographic controls. However, the aftereffects of this carelessness and negligence could potentially hamper further IoT spread. End users and merchants will be equally affected by the security breaches associated with IoT.

However, IoT devices, nodes, and protocols cannot handle heavy ciphers, which require high computing power and consume a lot of memory. Further research on lightweight cryptography is needed to efficiently enhance IoT security.

CHAPTER 7

Forensics and Trust in IoT

Introduction

IoT forensics and trust management are indirectly related to IoT security.

Forensics is an important subfield of security, which involves using specific skills, knowledge, and scientific methods to examine objects or substances involved in crimes.[73] *Digital forensics*, specifically, is the process of uncovering and interpreting electronic data.[74] IoT forensics, which is a branch of digital forensics, has its own characteristics that make it an attractive area for future research.

Trust is a basic prerequisite for smooth interaction between people. Trust is important in IT because, in many cases, these individuals are interacting without any physical contact. The huge mass of IoT, with lightweight entities spread over vast areas in different jurisdictions, makes trust management even more important.

---

[73] *See* http://dictionary.cambridge.org/dictionary/english/forensic

[74] https://www.techopedia.com/definition/27805/digital-forensics

1. Digital Forensics

The goal of digital forensics is to preserve data in its most original form while performing a structured investigation by collecting, identifying, and validating the data to reconstruct past events.

In the age of IT, cybercrimes are quite common. Many countries already have cyber laws in place and can rely on digital forensic techniques for implementation.

The process of digital forensics normally consists of the following five phases:

1. **Seizure.** The first step in the forensics process is seizing the area associated with the crime. Normally, this step is conducted by law enforcement agencies. If an incident occurs at an enterprise, hired security may also be involved in seizing the incident site.

2. **Acquisition of Evidence.** Next, the evidence must be acquired for investigation. Forensics experts normally use software tools to lock digital media so it cannot be modified further. Additionally, they typically create a copy of the digital media and take it into custody for further investigation and examination.

3. **Preservation of Evidence.** Before going ahead with the investigation, the evidence must be preserved by creating a digest for the digital media data. This digest is generated through a hash function to avoid tampering. The data may also be verified for its integrity at this, or at any other, stage of the process.

4. **Analysis.** Analysis is the essence of forensics; this step demands intelligence, experience, and hard work from investigators.

a. First, hypotheses are formulated; then, those hypotheses are correlated with the actual evidence trail. While some tools are available to facilitate the analysis, the most important inputs are human intelligence and intuition.

b. Also, since digital evidence is not the only evidence available to law enforcement agencies at this stage, the digital evidence is correlated with any physical evidence to form a full intelligence picture.

5. **Presentation and Reporting.** After having analyzed the evidence, the forensics team presents its findings to the jury or law enforcement hierarchy. While the technical intricacies of the overall forensic process do not need to be explained to non-technical people, the details should be available for presentation, if requested.

2. IoT Forensics

IoT has affected everything associated with the cyber world; cybercrimes, cyber laws, and digital forensics are no exception. *IoT forensics*, which is a branch of digital forensics, is the process of obtaining digital evidence of an event from IoT devices or networks in order to discover and prove causes of wrongdoing.

2.1 Characteristics of IoT forensics

Comparing digital forensics in the pre-IoT era with IoT forensics results in a few differences:

- **Digital Evidence.** Digital forensics in the pre-IoT era normally started with the acquisition of hard disk drives, mobile phones, network accessories, tertiary storage, USB flash drives, etc. However, in an IoT environment, in addition to the above-mentioned digital evidence, additional items, such as sensors, actuators, wearable devices, home appliances, and cloud storage would be included.

- **Evidence Preservation.** The pre-IoT era preserved digital evidence using general-purpose software like *write blockers*— tools that permit read-only access to data storage devices without compromising the integrity of the data—and standard applications such as FTK and EnCase. However, because the IoT environment is expected to be flooded with proprietary hardware and software, IoT forensics will likely require its own proprietary tools to address any potential problems this flood of proprietary hardware and software could cause.

- **Evidence Analysis.** Digital evidence used to be studied in detail, based on well-established principles and guidelines developed over years of forensic science research. Though IoT is an evolution of IT and Internet, its widespread deployment is swiftly taking place. This means that it will likely take even more time for the finer principles of IoT evidence analysis to be developed. New dimensions to cybercrimes in the IoT era will bring new experiences and practices for evidence collection and analysis.

- **Evidence Presentation.** Evidence acquisition, analysis, and results are typically reported through an oral presentation. However, the IoT era might see new forensic presentations, in the form of demonstrations on IoT mock-up systems, due to the complexity of the crimes.

2.2 Sources of Evidence in IoT

Digital evidence in an IoT environment can be found in one or more of the following entities:

- **IoT things**, including devices and sensors, can be examined; although, use of proprietary software tools and knowledge about the processes involved would be necessary.

- **Communication/network devices in WSANs**, including network nodes, access points, datagrams, and packets, are very important for tracing incidents. Access to audit logs can further enlighten forensic experts on the timings, routes, and extents of incidents.

- **External networks**, up to Internet infrastructure, can provide evidence collection.

2.3 Emerging Challenges for IoT Forensics

The particular characteristics of IoT forensics lead to several new challenges:

- **Tracing Evidence over Too Many Entities.** With crimes in IoT systems, it becomes extremely difficult to ascertain everyone at a crime scene or all of the entities with evidence. Trying to segregate or select entities from so many sensors and nodes would be an evidence collection challenge.

- **Understanding Crimes over IoT's Complex, Wide-Ranging Scope.** IoT's widespread scope, colossal number of entities, integration with the cloud, multiple workflows, and similar features make it a tremendously complex system. Forensic engineers must understand the entire IoT system in order to examine crime scenes and to collect evidence.

- **Varying Laws and Jurisdictions.** The wide range of IoT deployment spread over different states and countries adds more constraints for forensics. Applicable laws, jurisdictions, network idiosyncrasies, etc., might vary within a single crime's effective area. For example, if a cybercrime were committed across multiple states, a forensics engineer who needs to collect evidence across those states would have to be in compliance with all of the states' laws and regulations.

- **Collecting Evidence without Affecting Its Condition.** Collecting evidence without affecting the condition of the evidence is already an existing forensic challenge. IoT will only increase this challenge because of the complex types and locations of evidence spread over so many entities.

- **Dearth of Forensic Tools.** Tools for efficient evidence acquisition and preservation are vital for IoT forensics. However, this is a challenge in an environment with so many different types of entities in the market, often with proprietary software.

- **Preserving Environmental Evidence.** A very peculiar issue of IoT forensics is the collection and preservation of evidence related to environmental conditions like temperature, humidity, wind speed, etc., because IoT devices usually have sensors that may collect this information.

- **Wide-Ranging Awareness from Forensic Experts.** IoT's wide scope will likely involve many routine life processes. This means IoT forensics investigations will likely require knowledge about the specific fields in which a crime was committed.

3. IoT Trust Management

For interactions involving some give and take, trust is a necessity. For example, if an IoT device were to automatically authorize some transaction, both the device owner and the vendor would want the authorization to be legitimate. Trust can be achieved either by proving one's credentials to others, personally or through some other already trusted authority. Trust, in information security, can be established for a party after authentication and authorization, confirmed with the association of a token.

Trust management in IT carries extra importance in cases of automated processes, such as financial transactions and access to critical resources. Because the parties involved in transactions are not interacting face to face, the trust has to be established through electronic means. Relevant tokens used to confirm trust include tickets, keys, tags, sessions IDs, etc.

IoT has taken automated transactions to new heights. Billions of entities interact with each other, with even more entities added every day. Topology changes are routine. Such an ad hoc and fluid scenario adds weight to trust management.

3.1 Challenges in IoT Trust Management

The huge number of entities and transactions and the level of automation IoT offers add significance to IoT trust management. However, aside from the basic characteristics of IoT, IoT trust management also faces finer challenges:

- **Need for a Common Method for Entity Identification.** IoT entities are being manufactured by different vendors, sometimes with proprietary features. IoT access networks are deployed for automating a wide range of processes and services in different topologies and security settings. This huge number of entities, networked in so many varying environments, requires complex methods for establishing trust in order for the entities to interact with each other and communicate through public, global networks.

- **Expensive External Security Measures.** IoT entities are typically lightweight, in terms of computing power, memory, and battery life. Built-in security features can make entities expensive and heavy. However, when insecure things are connected to form IoT, WSAN and security protections must be added later. This makes trust management complex, especially since certification authorities for trust management must be external.

- **Limited or No User Insight into Data Collection.** Proper IoT automation allows processes to operate with little to no user interaction. However, users cannot be expected to monitor continuous streams of data. This lack of continuous user oversight means that the sensors and entities operating on a user's behalf cannot be inherently trusted.

- **Combinations of Non-Sensitive Data.** Problems may arise in the IoT environment when otherwise non-sensitive chunks of information can be combined to become sensitive. Various separate pieces of data, once combined, could become health information or other personal user information. Trust management mechanisms might not be prepared for such scenarios.

- **Users Unaware of Compromised Devices.** With so many sensors silently doing their jobs, users could easily lose track of all of the devices installed in their homes. This means that, in the case of a hacked device, users might not know about the compromise for quite some time. Hacked devices are not just a dangerous prospect for user privacy; they can also be used for perpetrating attacks (e.g., DDoS botnet attacks) while masquerading as the user's trusted entity.

- **Back-doored Devices.** Recent events have confirmed that countries do collect data from common users through backdoors in firmware, graphic controllers, network cards, etc. This makes privacy protection very difficult for the IoT environment, along with trust.

3.2 Creating Trust in IoT Environment

Trust establishment and management are important aspects of the IoT environment. Principles for creating trust in IoT are similar to trust-building in real life.[75]

- **Identification.** The foremost principle of establishing trust is proving one's identity. All IoT entities should be uniquely identified through a universal identification system. No one should be able to change an entity's identity. Attackers should not be able to masquerade as a legitimate entity.

- **Benign Intention/Behavior.** An identified entity is not necessarily a trusted entity. An identified entity can also, knowingly or unknowingly, be part of a malicious agenda. Attacks through botnets are one example where authenticated and authorized entities unknowingly participate in malicious activity.

  In IoT, the mass number of devices makes such attacks even more devastating. IoT needs a mechanism to assess an entity's behavior and determine its intentions, in order to build trust.

- **Predictability.** Trusted IoT entities should typically operate with predictable behavior. Predictability is only possible if users can know the full scope of an entity's functionality. Entity operations or activities should not surprise users or other entities (e.g., a smart refrigerator ordering unwanted food); otherwise, trust may be lost.

- **Transparency.** Closely related to predictability is the notion of transparency. Device operations should be transparent to allow users and other entities to clearly see what the device

---

[75] Christof Jungo, Integrity and Trust in the Internet of Things, Swisscom Ltd, December 2015.

is doing. Actions designed to obscure transparency, such as falsification of records or misuse of data, will break established levels of trust.

- **Repute.** In the real world, a positive reputation is established after multiple positive interactions with others. Because the IoT world is a virtualization of the real world, the same process applies; entities should be able to build a positive reputation after positive interactions. However, when reputation becomes a factor, identity masquerading or spoofing can have even more devastating effects.

- **Continuity.** The trust established among entities should be constant, based on the outcome of continued, benign operation and authenticated behavior. As in the real world, manufacturers that develop reliable products are considered trustworthy. Similarly, the IoT environment should also rely on records of benign behavior to create trust continuity and consistency.

4. Trust Modeling in IoT

Traditional access control methods may not be suitable for the dynamic and decentralized IoT environment, as the types and number of entities are not known in advance. Rich literature exists addressing trust modeling issues of IoT.[76] Several, important trust models have already been proposed.

4.1 Trust-Based Access Control for IoT

A trust-based access control framework should be able to calculate trust scores using factors like experience, knowledge, and recommendation.

---

[76] Kai-Di Chang and Jiann-Liang Chen, "A Survey of Trust Management in WSNs, Internet of Things and Future Internet." *KSII Transactions on Internet and Information Systems* 6 no. 1 (January 2012).

The trust scores that are obtained should then be appended with the access control permissions. The framework consists of three layers:[77]

- **Device Layer.** This layer includes all of the things in IoT: sensors, actuators, and the WSAN's network devices and nodes.

- **Request Layer.** This is the layer where the trust score is calculated by evaluating various attributes of the entities: experience, repute, behavior, etc.

- **Access Control Layer.** This is the processing layer that decides, on the basis of trust score, what access control privileges are available to an entity.

4.2 Trust Evaluation in IoT

Because IoT aims to automate daily processes, it can be considered a service provider for its users. However, trust management operates as a supplementary service to IoT systems, providing authenticity of IoT's services to users. This perspective results in another three-layered approach to trust evaluation.[78]

- **Sensor Layer.** This layer includes all sensors in the constantly communicating IoT devices.

- **Infrastructure Layer.** Also termed the *core layer*, this layer provides a platform to the sensor layer in the form of WSAN and the Internet. It includes all network devices and nodes as part of IoT access networks and the global network.

---

[77] Fenye Bao and Chen Ing-Ray, "Dynamic Trust Management for Internet of Things Applications." Proceedings of the 2012 International Workshop on Self-Aware Internet of Things. ACM, 2012.

[78] Jing Pei Wang, et al. "Distributed Trust Management Mechanism for the Internet of Things," *Applied Mechanics and Materials* 347 (Trans Tech Publications, 2013).

- **Application Layer.** This layer consists of various applications, interfaces, and distributed systems.

4.3 An Integrated Scheme for Trust Management

Another proposed trust model guards user security with a combination of position-aware and identity-aware information and history.[79] This allows users to acquire trust knowledge for entities and requested services. This model defines three zones of trust for entities and services: high, medium, and low. An entity or service's associated zone defines how it may be further authenticated.

- **High Trust Zone.** If an entity already possesses a high level of trust, then no further authentication is required. This is the most trusted level an entity can achieve.

- **Medium Trust Zone.** Entities or users in this zone have to present personal identification numbers for authentication and login. Still, this is a fairly trusted zone of operation.

- **Low Trust Zone.** Entities unable to acquire sufficient trust are placed in this zone. These entities need to provide biometric credentials to take part in communication.

4.4 Context-Aware Multi-Service Trust

This model establishes trust level of entities by collecting past behavioral statistics from adjacent nodes.[80] This decentralized approach requires cooperation among nodes in an IoT environment. Trust is established by the help of first- and secondhand knowledge about an entity. This model includes four phases.

---

[79] Yang Liu, et al. "An Integrated Scheme Based on Service Classification in Pervasive Mobile Services," *International Journal of Communication Systems* 25.9 (2012): 1178–1188.
[80] Yosra Ben Saied, et al. "Trust Management System Design for the Internet of Things: A Context-Aware and Multi-Service Approach," *Computers & Security* 39 (2013): 351–365.

1. Collect trust information of available nodes.
2. Establish a mechanism for collaborating with other nodes.
3. Update its own information from the past experiences.
4. Allocate a trust score or level to each node after every new interaction.

5. Open Problems in IoT Trust Management

While different trust models try to address trust management in IoT, the subject still requires more attention. The following issues remain open problems in IoT trust management.[81]

- **Need for Trust Negotiation Language.** There is a dire need to develop a language for IoT trust negotiation. IoT characteristics make pre-IoT trust management models fall short of handling trust issues in IoT, especially with various IoT interoperability scenarios. This makes a new trust negotiating language that is expressive enough to support the needs of various interoperability scenarios a critical need for IoT.

- **Defining an Object Identity Management System.** Identity management of IoT entities is far from comprehensive. Many different attributes are associated with device identity, thereby adding to the complexity. A universal system of identification for IoT entities should be accepted and adopted by all manufacturers and software vendors.

- **Developing Trust Negotiating Mechanism.** Many different trust-negotiating mechanisms have been proposed for IoT. For efficient and standardized trust negotiation among entities, with minimum overhead, a single mechanism must be adopted.

---

[81] Sabrina Sicari, et al. "Security, Privacy and Trust in Internet of Things: The Road Ahead," *Computer Networks* 76 (2015): 146–164.

Conclusion

Forensics and trust management issues in IoT can be understood only after appreciating their basic implications in the pre-IoT era. These areas of IT were well-established in the pre-IoT period, but they require further progress in the IoT era. Refinements in the field of digital forensics and mechanisms for efficient trust management are necessary, due to IoT idiosyncrasies. Colossal numbers of entities, most of which are lightweight; ad hoc access networks; large volumes of data; amalgamation of technologies; and vast coverage areas all necessitate revisiting forensics and trust management.

While efforts are being made to align digital forensics and trust management with IoT progress, current efforts are falling short. IoT still needs a consistent and mature way forward.

CHAPTER 8
Regulatory Compliance in IoT

Introduction

Organizations should make their systems compliant with information security standards. Compliance not only hardens organizations against prevailing attack vectors; it also protects organizations against legal repercussions in case of a security breach. Because compliance is such an important aspect of the modern-day business environment, it is important to understand what makes IoT compliance different from compliance in pre-IoT times.

IoT compliance is focused on two major aspects. The first studies challenges involved in making security standards for IoT. The second deals with the challenges faced by organizations implementing those standards.

Formulating new security standards or revamping existing security standards requires understanding the IoT implications. The enormous scope of IoT, encompassing various industries, makes security standards complex. When enterprises attempt compliance, the complex and wide-scoped standards become difficult to understand and implement.

1. Compliance

TechTarget defines "compliance" as "either a state of being in accordance with established guidelines or specifications, or the process of becoming so." [82]

Compliance does not always provide necessary security against all prevailing threats. An enterprise fully compliant with prevailing standards may still be subjected to attacks. However, because noncompliance to relevant laws and prevailing standards leads to legal complications, compliance carries a lot of weight in the business world.

2. Notable Security Standards

Numerous standards present compliance requirements for industries to implement. The difficulty of compliance for each of these requirements is expected to increase in the IoT era. Notable standards include:

- **HIPAA.** The Health Insurance Portability and Accountability Act (HIPAA) came into force in the United States in 1996. The act was created for safeguarding data privacy and medical information after a series of hacks into health insurance providers resulted in multiple data breaches of health records.

  HIPAA consists of five sections to be implemented by anyone holding medical records. All healthcare businesses are required to be compliant with HIPAA in order to ensure privacy of patients' personal information.

- **PCI DSS.** As a result of numerous credit card frauds, Payment Card Industry Data Security Standard (PCI DSS) was devised by major credit card brands. PCI DSS applies to anyone handling credit card payments. It aims to address fraud issues

---

[82] http://searchdatamanagement.techtarget.com/definition/compliance

by protecting cardholders' data. PCI DSS has six sections, with a total of twelve compliance requirements.

- **ISO-27001.** ISO-27001 helps organizations secure their information assets. This standard was published in 2013 by International Organization for Standardization (ISO) to provide guidelines for an information security management system. Organizations that abide by ISO-27001 specifications receive a certificate of compliance from an accredited certification body. ISO-27001 includes ten short clauses and set of security controls, along with an annex of objectives.

3. IoT Compliance Challenges

The growing scope and increasing user base of IoT have serious ramifications for regulatory compliance. Mandatory compliance starts with formulating standards to be implemented by organizations.

3.1 Difficulty in Formulating the Standards for Compliance

- **Revision of Existing Standards.** Existing standards for various industries might not suffice for projects under IoT. IoT offers more connectivity, encompasses many more entities, uses big data, relies on the cloud and ad hoc diverse access networks, etc. These peculiarities require existing standards to be refined accordingly.

  For example, many standards recommend installing software firewalls at the user end. However, the lightweight nature of typical IoT devices, which causes them to be resource constrained, may not allow them to handle firewall software.

- **Widespread Scope.** IoT offers a wide variety of services in different fields. A single IoT project could automate processes dealing with multiple industries. Therefore, standards from different industries will need to be adopted and conformed for this interaction. IoT cannot be taken as a single industry with regards to compliance. A single IoT project may have to abide by some specific governmental regulations, implement PCI DSS for payments, and address regulations pertaining to other industries in its scope.

- **Combination of Technologies.** IoT deployment implements many technologies. The network infrastructure is a mix of the existing global Internet and IoT access networks, based on WSAN technologies. Big data analytics and cloud computing, for storage or more services, also form part of IoT. Formulating compliance and monitoring standards encompassing all of these technologies is another challenge.

- **Varying Jurisdictions.** The widespread scope of IoT makes it common for IoT projects to encompass areas with varied legal jurisdictions and cyber laws. These laws might change compliance requirements and therefore require close attention by those formulating IoT compliance standards.

3.2 Challenges in Achieving Compliance

- **Diversity in Hardware and Software.** IoT sensors and actuators, WSAN technologies, network devices, etc., consist of diverse and sometimes proprietary hardware and software. This diverse nature of various IoT bits and pieces makes it difficult to conform them to standards.

- **Huge Number of Dynamic Devices.** The number of entities in IoT are not only huge in number but are constantly increasing and changing their locations. The changing topologies and built-in ad hocism of IoT further complicates compliance, both accomplishment and monitoring.

- **Limitations of Lightweight Components.** For IoT, conformance to standards at the individual entity level may be extremely difficult or impossible. As highlighted earlier, not all regulatory precautions can be implemented at the edge locations of IoT entities, due to their limited computing power, low memory, and meager or non-existent storage.

- **Difficulty in Upgrades and Updates.** Compliance requirements that include updating software or upgrading sensors, actuators, or hardware for each IoT entity may require ages to complete. Compatibility and operational issues may also arise.

- **Complex Vulnerability and Risk Assessment.** IoT uses so many brands of hardware and software that vulnerability and risk assessments would be daunting tasks for enterprise information security departments. However, information security management starts from these assessments, which must be documented for compliance requirements.

4. IoT Compliance Guidelines

Compliance implementation in IoT can be achieved by abiding by the following guidelines.

- **Documentation.** To start with any IoT project, it is imperative to document the planning and implementation phases. All diagrams, layouts, engineering drawings, network architectures, etc., must be kept safe. Changes incorporated during the course of implementation or maintenance should also be recorded, along with necessary authorization stamps.

   Comprehensive and clear documentation is the first requirement for any compliance mechanism. Documentation would also be a valuable source for people involved in working for compliance with any future standards.

Without proper documentation, IoT deployment could be a mess. Modifications in a running IoT system would be highly complex, and a lack of proper documentation could take the system into an unstable and insecure state.

- **Testing Facility.** Project operation and maintenance can be reasonably streamlined if all controls are tested before they are brought into the production environment. This testing would support a compliance monitoring mechanism for the company's internal auditors and security professionals. Any IoT initiatives should be tested for security controls in the test facility before rollout.

- **Security Management System.** Huge systems, like IoT, need thorough security management. All IoT entities should be monitored through a central control to ensure they are operating properly. Such central management can spread cooperating tentacles over an IoT project's deployment area in order to create better and easier compliance monitoring mechanisms.

- **Incident Reporting System.** Just like a central security management system, there is a need to establish a centralized incident and event management system. Security Incident and Event Management (SIEM) solutions[83] can normally address all aspects of security management, including live incident reporting and event management. SIEM systems are essential to IoT compliance monitoring.

- **Partners' Compliance Reports.** The IoT environment is an interoperable organization of multiple working systems made up of entities with many different vendors. Cloud services, big data analytics, WSAN providers, etc., are actually full-fledged

---

[83] An approach to security management in which data is aggregated and analyzed in real time to determine if any action should be taken.

operational projects run by different organizations. In IoT, one organization may be dependent on multiple others for its services. This necessitates a level of trust among partners where compliance efforts must be shared among cooperating organizations to achieve unified compliance.

- **Periodic Compliance Assessment.** Conformity to international security standards is not a onetime need. Enterprises aiming for IoT compliance should periodically use internal resources to perform compliance assessments. A local compliance monitoring team, maybe within an organization's information security department, is much needed. Such a team would not only improve enterprise security posture; it would also take care of legal issues related to compliance checks.

5. Some IoT Compliance Standards

IT security should use security standards to comprehensively cover IoT-related aspects.

- **ISO/IEC JTC 1/SWG 5.** ISO/IEC JTC 1/SWG 5 IoT is a special working group for developing IoT security standards.[84] The group has already created some terms of reference, including identifying market requirements and IoT standardization gaps. Standardization gaps include gateway security, network function virtualization security, management and measurement of IoT security, open source assurance and security, IoT risk assessment techniques, privacy and big data, application security guidance for IoT, and IoT incident response and guidance.

- **NERC CIP.** North American Electric Reliability Corporation's Critical Infrastructure Protection (NERC CIP) standards

---

[84] ISO/IEC JTC 1. Establishment of SWG on Internet of Things (IoT). December 11, 2012.

address electric generation and distribution systems employed in IoT.[85]

- **NIST CPS.** NIST released its framework for cyber physical systems (CPS) called NIST CPS.[86] This framework helps the CPS industry create security standards for protecting information and assets.

Conclusion

Regulatory compliance is a very important aspect of the enterprise business market. Enterprises may initially see compliance as a defense against legal repercussions from security breaches. However, if an enterprise starts making compliance efforts without first plugging security loopholes, it may cost much more.

IoT compliance is no exception to this rule. In the IoT environment, enterprises first need to understand the finer details of IoT security and then focus on how to be compliant.

---

[85] www.nerc.com/pa/Stand/Pages/CIPStandards.aspx

[86] https://www.nist.gov/el/cyber-physical-systems

CHAPTER 9

Identity and Access Management in IoT

Introduction

Identity and access management solutions, known as IAM, provide the linchpin for system security. IAM has been used for operational systems even before the days of IT and connectivity.

IAM starts with the unique identification of an entity. Once an entity has been identified, rights and privileges are issued to the particular entity to determine how it can access information and what information it can access. This is called *authorization*. With authorization controls in place, IAM should be able to issue some sort of token to the entity, based on its access privileges. The entity can then use the token to enter the system and perform its routine, assigned tasks. While the entity works, its operation is monitored and logged by IAM. This monitoring mechanism keeps entities accountable and assures that they cannot deny any actions they committed.

Understanding the basics of IAM provides a basis for discussing IoT peculiarities that affect traditional IAM implementation. These peculiarities highlight the areas of IAM that need special attention in the IoT era, including identity management, authentication, and authorization. IoT idiosyncrasies can be used to create succinct guidelines for setting up IAM solutions in the IoT realm.

1. What Is IAM?

IAM aims to manage entity authentication and authorization to access various assets and resources. With an IAM system in place, organizations can enforce access rules as per some governing policy, with regards to permissions granted to entities for usage of resources.

Webopedia has defined IAM as "a framework of policies and technologies for ensuring that the proper people in an enterprise have appropriate access to technology resources." [87] IAM also determines which hardware and software individuals need to access.

While IAM typically does not result in tangible differences for systems, it does result in sizable, long-term improvement in security posture. The absence of IAM makes an administrator's job difficult, if not impossible, in environments where employees are permitted to use varied personal devices.

There are three distinct parts of IAM:

- Authentication or identity management
- Authorization or access control management
- A centralized directory service, in which user credentials are stored, along with their associated permissions

    The system should also have a mechanism for user account/ profile creation and management. Administrators should also have the option to set up rights and permissions for particular users or groups of users.

---

[87] http://www.webopedia.com/TERM/I/iam-identity-and-access-management. html

2. IDoT—Where IAM Meets IoT

IoT implementation and deployment are complex, with IoT's huge number of entities, large volumes of data, amalgamation of technologies, etc. The same factors that make IoT complex also add to the intricacies of IAM in the IoT environment. IAM in an IoT environment is called *Identity of Things* (IDoT). IDoT differs from standard IAM in several ways.

- **Different Relationships.** IDoT is not limited to relationships between human beings and devices. Rather, IDoT encompasses IoT's large number of devices. In IoT, authentication and authorization challenges are extended to the physical entities forming part of the overall system. All entities must be uniquely identified, with rights and roles for each thing correctly defined and assigned.

- **Varying Lifecycles.** Lifespans of IoT entities vary from as little as a few hours to as long as a person's entire life. For example, a shipment's lifecycle ends when it reaches the destination. However, the lifecycle of an individual's social security account lasts for the individual's lifetime. Different lifecycles for such a huge number of entities have serious repercussions for access management. For example, if the varying lifecycles of IoT devices are not monitored, it is easier for nefarious actors to gain illegal access through devices masquerading as non-existent entities.

- **Potentially Ineffective Biometrics.** For IoT entities that are not human beings, biometric authentication may not work. Therefore, two-factor or multifactor authentication has different implications in the IoT environment. Authentication routines become difficult because of how much the uniqueness of entities matters in IoT. IoT needs a system where entities could be unquestionably, uniquely identified. Only then should additional permissions be set.

- **Performance Issues.** IDoT platforms need to manage millions of identities with thousands or more transactions per second. A pre-IoT IAM system might simply fail due to performance issues trying to handle such big numbers. In the IoT era, IAM systems should focus on lightweight software routines to identify, authenticate, and authorize entities.

- **Need for Continuity and Context-Based Security.** Time spent with pre-IoT systems has already revealed that authentication at session initiation is not good enough. Entity actions should be repeatedly authenticated. The need for additional security is even more pronounced in the IoT era. Many IoT entities are never going to be switched off or logged off from the system and may have been authenticated once they were switched on long ago. IDoT needs to use varied authentication types, including contextual identity, adaptive risk, and multifactor, both at initiation and during operation.

- **Privacy Concerns.** With so many entities interacting, privacy concerns for IDoT include the amount of user data is being shared and whether user consent has been sought. IDoT platforms must offer users various options for privacy preferences, including consent to share data.

3. Main Challenges for IDoT

The challenges posed by IoT for IAM systems fall into several broad areas.

- **Initial Authentication and Authorization.** IAM mechanisms should be able to quickly add new devices. The authorization mechanism should be risk free, adaptive, and context based.

However, even with these requirements, the system should not be resource intensive.

- **Safe Sharing.** IoT demands sharing: resources, data, devices, etc. Without sharing, IoT cannot benefit its users. IDoT should be able to allow information and resources to be shared without compromising authorization permissions.

- **Maintaining Privacy.** In IoT, entities are continuously sensing data and forwarding it to controlling systems for automation and active engagement. Customer privacy must be maintained throughout this process. IDoT systems should be able to give users control and consent regarding the data they share.

4. IoT Identity Management

Identity management begins with assigning objects with unique identifiers. Other than uniqueness, the identifiers should also highlight the device's brand and type. For example, a typical identifier may include manufacturer name, serial number, deployment date, etc.

Based on an entity's identification, its permissions—authorizations to perform various activities or access to certain resources—are set. Duplicating or tampering identities will lead to incorrect permissions.

After an identifier has been assigned at the time of an entity's creation, the device can be booted up. Devices should be trusted not to carry some false identity or spoof someone else. The manufacturing process can address these concerns by embossing a serial number or using some counter mechanism. The same serial number should also be included in the device's ROM. Public Key Infrastructure (PKI) can also be utilized for certificates.

Overall, identity management security should address the following aspects:

- No new entities should be created without secure identification, ideally preventing rogue devices from becoming part of the system.
- Entity masquerading should not be possible.
- Trust through cryptographic mechanisms should be established.

After entities are booted up, their communications must be secured. For this purpose, attributes or credentials must be enabled for the entity. Preferably, authentication through certificates should be managed.

Some IAM systems may include a requirement that allows administrators to locally access device identity. Devices may be spread over a large area, but IAM should provide access to the entities in an organized manner.

An efficient IAM system will be involved with device creation, startup, and communication. However, IAM should also continually monitor the entities and their behavior to see if they possess any properties contrary to their credentials.

Additionally, IAM systems should be able to periodically update device credentials. The IoT environment may seem to make this a daunting task, but the security is much needed. The short life of security certificates provides less leverage to attackers who have already entered a system.

Finally, once accounts are no longer required, IAM systems should be able to delete them.

5. Authentication in IoT

The biggest challenge for IoT authentication is the shift from human-centric authentication to the authentication of devices and things. Before any interaction or data exchange between IoT entities, both parties should correctly authenticate each other.

IoT messaging protocols support using different authentication credentials:

- Passwords
- Cryptographic keys
- Authorization certificates
- Biometrics

5.1 Password Authentication

Usernames and passwords are a very basic arrangement for authentication, but they are not ideal for ensuring authentication security. For usernames and passwords to be effective, additional controls must be added to the authentication system. Such precautions include the following:

- Additional policies should be implemented to ensure periodic password changes.
- Device activity should be monitored, even after successful authentication, through an efficient system. Highly privileged entities—for example, those containing financial or medical information, should be constantly watched and scrutinized.
- Devices and networks should be earmarked relying only on username and password authentication as less trusted regions.

Some protocols, such as MQTT (MQ Telemetry Transport, or Message Queue Telemetry Transport), offer usernames and passwords as their only authentication option. MQTT is a lightweight messaging protocol that can be used over TCP/IP networks. However, managing usernames and passwords through MQTT does not offer any further security for transmitting credentials over communication media. These and other further security concerns must be addressed:

- Some cryptographic security of these credentials while on the move must be employed.

- Secure storage of these credentials is a daunting task.
- Managing a huge number of credentials would be required, as each entity would have one set.
- Passwords need to be efficiently managed during the complete life of each device.

5.2 Cryptographic Authentication

Cryptography is useful for devising authentication mechanisms. For example, with a username and password-only combination, the username and password could be secured through the TLS protocol. Other cryptographic mechanisms can also be employed for authentication:

- **MAC (Message Authentication Code).** Using a pre-shared MAC algorithm key, a sender can generate a MAC against a message and append it to the message. Once the receiving party receives the message, it uses its key to also calculate the MAC of the message. If the obtained MAC is same as appended by the sender, this means that the sender possesses the correct key. That way, the sender is believed to be authenticated.

- **Digital Certificates.** Digital certificates provide an even better method of authentication than MAC because they also provide non-repudiation. In this case, the sender appends its digital certificate to the message using its own private key. Now, this digital certificate can be verified by the receiver by using the sender's public key, which is available in a central repository. Verification of the sender's digital signature authenticates the sender. Additionally, because only the sender holds its private key, the sender cannot deny sending this message, which is important in the IoT environment with respect to automated financial transactions. This non-repudiation aspect was missing in MAC because the secret key held by the sender was also held by the receiver.

5.3 Biometric Authentication

Authentication through biometric properties can act as either a single or secondary authentication mechanism in IoT. Biometric properties such as voice, fingerprinting, and iris scans can be digitally recognized for access control management.

6. PKI (Public Key Infrastructure) in IoT

Public key cryptography works through public and private key pairs associated with entities. The private keys are only known to the respective entities; the public keys are publically available within the network. PKI ensures that public keys are correct and properly associated with respective entities.

Any message encrypted by one key of a public-private key pair can be decrypted by the other key. For example, if sender A encrypts a message with its private key, the message can be decrypted by anyone who receives the message and can access A's public key from a public repository. That way, anyone decrypting the message can be sure of both its origin authenticity and its integrity. On the other hand, if A sends a message by encrypting it with B's public key, the message can be decrypted only by B's private key, which is possessed only by B. In this case, A can be sure that the message only gets to B. In both of these scenarios, it is important that the public key repository have the correct public keys for all entities in the system. PKI systems are used for this purpose.

A PKI system consists of the following components:

- **Digital Certificate.** Digital certificates for IoT entities are like ID cards. A common public-key cryptography certificate used in various current Internet protocols, like TLS/SSL, is the X.509 certificate, based on the X.509 standard. However, other standards may be used instead.

- **Certification Authority (CA).** The CA issues digital certificates to clients on a network and assists clients in verifying digital certificates through their public keys. A client entity seeking a digital certificate for itself submits a request, along with its attributes, to the CA. The CA then generates a public-private key pair for that client. Clients keep private keys in their custody as a digital certificate; public keys are kept with the CA and are made available to other parties for verification. For better security, the private key is stored in secure, removable storage.

  For huge networks, like the Internet and IoT, having only one CA is impractical, as it would be a single point of failure. The solution for certificate management would be a complete CA hierarchy under one root CA.

- **Registration Authority (RA).** CAs sometimes get help from RAs to provide necessary scrutiny of client entities requesting for digital certificates.

- **Certificate Management System (CMS).** CMS incorporates both CAs and RAs. CMS performs functions related to certificate management like issuing, revoking, suspending, and renewing.

7. Authorization in IoT

Once IoT entities have been uniquely identified and authenticated, the next challenge is assigning permissions and roles. Mere entry into the system does not mean that an entity can read, write, or perform any other tasks within the system. Authorization, or access control, methods ensure that entities can only access information as per their roles or permissions. For example, in an IoT, system, only trusted, authorized parties should be allowed to update an entity's software, access an entity's sensor data, or command an actuator.

IoT has very clear requirements for authorization, but a few IoT peculiarities add challenges to authorization in an IoT environment:

- Low power requirements of devices
- Limited bandwidth between IoT access networks and the global Internet
- Distributed system
- Ad hocism in WSANs
- Huge number of entities with large volumes of data

The immediate implication of IoT peculiarities is that traditional access control methods must be thoroughly analyzed before deployment in an IoT environment. These controls include the following:

- Access Control List (ACL)[88]
- Attribute-Based Access Control (ABAC)[89]
- Discretionary Access Control (DAC)[90]
- History-Based Access Control (HBAC)[91]
- Identity-Based Access Control (IBAC)[92]
- Mandatory Access Control (MAC)[93]
- Organization-Based Access Control (OrBAC)[94]
- Role-Based Access Control (RBAC)[95]
- Rule-Based Access Control (RAC)[96]

Access control methods in IoT can be implemented in either a centralized or a distributed manner.

---

[88] A table that states which permissions are attached to an object and specifies which users are authorized to access that object.

[89] Access is based on user, resource, and environmental attributes.

[90] Access is based on a subject's identity or group membership.

[91] Access is based on past security actions.

[92] Access is based on whether a name is included on the ACL.

[93] Access to a system is controlled by an operating system under the control of an administrator.

[94] Access is based on a system in which security policy is designed for and by an organization.

[95] Access is based on a user's role within an organization.

[96] Access is based on whether a request for access is allowed by predetermined rule.

8. Recommended Strategies for IAM in IoT

An understanding of identity management and access controls provides the groundwork for recommended strategies for IAM solutions in an IoT environment.

- **Amalgamate IoT into existing IAM.** This strategy starts with the prerequisite that all entities be uniquely identified through some standard, informative naming convention throughout their lifecycle. Next is a comprehensive registration process, followed by establishing authentication and authorization mechanisms based on the organization's needs. Finally, this solution should include a defined mechanism for administrator access to the devices.

- **Protect entities with strong admin passwords.** Default administrator passwords must be streamed. A scheme for strong administrator passwords should be strictly followed.[97]

- **Implement Identity Relationship Management (IRM).** Traditional IAM solutions handle internal identification, authentication, and authorization mechanisms. By contrast, IRM not only handles access privileges of internal employees and enclosed machines; it goes on to encompass customers, partners, and entities, irrespective of their geographic locations.

- **Dictate authorization rules according to threat scenarios.** No standard IAM solution can address every organization's needs. Solutions should be based on the specific threat matrix faced by each company's business environment. Hypothesizing threat scenarios or attack vectors allows an IAM solution to be properly planned based on the surroundings.

---

[97] For example, by requiring passwords of a certain length that must include letters (uppercase and lowercase), numbers, and symbols.

- **Shift to IPv6.** While IPv6 has been available for a while, many organizations are still content with IPv4, meaning IPv4 IoT devices could still be around for years. Therefore, organizations should not only transition to IPv6 as soon as possible, but they should also ensure communication management between IPv6 and IPv4 devices.

- **Get PKI support.** With large-scale IoT deployments, it is imperative to use PKI for IAM. Digital certificates must be used for device authentication and negotiations, and all PKI services—certificate issuance, checking, revocation, trust management, etc.—should be implemented and utilized.

- **Examine device usage statistics going to vendors.** Vendors of IoT devices typically collect usage statistics from their products, mostly for improvements and support services. However, with so many different IoT entities coming from different vendors, authorization mechanisms for streamlining such data collection must be followed.

- **Establish AAA servers.** AAA servers provide authentication, authorization, and accounting services for businesses. In the IoT environment, AAA servers should manage access control for outsiders as well as internal entities, customers, partners, etc.

- **Manage privileged rights.** Security obtained from an IAM solution can be compromised if administrative rights, privileges, and sessions are not properly monitored and managed. Mismanagement in closing disused privileged accounts and services and not abiding by the law of least privilege can be detrimental to enterprise security.

- **Oversee inventories.** Another important aspect of IAM is managing inventories and ownership records of all types of entities and assets. Entities should be categorized based on sensitivity to security and associated risks.

- **Build human and device relationships.** While IoT has more hardware entities than human beings, most of the entities are associated with some human being. IAM solutions should try to map humans with their related devices and things, and, therefore, ease management access to the devices.

- **Utilize IoT protocols' controls.** Various IoT standards and protocols have built-in controls to facilitate entity authentication. All such controls must be known to the administrators, and they must be used when required.

Conclusion

No system, IoT-based or not, is complete without an IAM solution. IDoT requires comprehensive IAM solutions in IoT-enabled systems.

IDoT deals with unique identification and authentication of entities in an IoT environment. The huge number of entities in IoT poses a serious challenge to unique identification. Moreover, the inability to use biometric properties for many IoT entities raises issues of accurate authentication.

After authentication comes setting the correct rights, permissions, or privileges for entities. User rights management can be very tricky for IoT entities that are never switched off, periodically change their location, and have varied lifecycles.

The IoT landscape has brought serious challenges for IAM solution providers. Further research into cryptographic controls and PKI is necessary, but the lightweight nature of most IoT entities must also be considered. Refined and lightweight PKI solutions, specifically tailored to IoT needs, seem to be the answer for the future of IDoT.

CHAPTER 10

Incident Response Management in IoT

Introduction

Incident response management has been practiced even before the IT revolution. In any industry, planning for troublesome occurrences saves time, resources, and effort.

Many cybersecurity incident response teams (CSIRTs) operate around the world. Some CSIRTs are linked with each other for incident sharing and posing a coherent defense to attackers.

In the IoT era, more emphasis is placed on incident response and handling mechanisms. The IoT world is characterized by billions of connected entities communicating among each other and generating enormous volumes of data. IoT also encompasses big data analytics and cloud computing. This massive system is likely beyond the monitoring capabilities of existing incident response teams.

Though related to traditional incident management, incident response management in IoT includes several peculiar, finer aspects. Incident response management in IoT requires deliberate planning and careful rollout, with the simultaneous deployment of IoT solutions.

1. Fundamentals of Incident Management

Incident response management was recognized as an important pillar of information security well before IoT. Implementing all possible security controls does not completely relieve any organization from security worries. Incidents occasionally happen even at highly security-conscious and well-protected organizations.

Because untoward incidents will continue to happen in spite of safeguards, reactions to incidents are of paramount importance. Quick and timely responses to security incidents can save an organization time, effort, money, legal issues, and reputation damage. Such responses are possible only if organizations have working incident response management systems. Incident response mechanisms should be designed to reliably handle security incident situations by limiting damaging effects and enabling recovery to a stable, calm state as soon as possible.

Incident response management best operates when it caters to the peculiarities of the prevailing environment and encompasses probable threat scenarios. Incident management in an IoT environment includes its own specifics.

2. Peculiarities in IoT Incident Management

When compared with the standard incident response management cycle (as illustrated in figure 10.1), there are no general differences in incident response management in an IoT environment. However, incident management in IoT must be prepared to handle newer incidents and threat scenarios. Examples could include the following:

- **Driverless Car Hack.** A driverless car moving to its programmed destination could be targeted, hacked by an attacker, and driven to a location other than its destination. The car's controls should be able sense the deviation, determine a probable hack, and report it to the control station. The incident should also be monitored by the security operation center (SOC), quickly sent up the chain to the CSIRT, and alerted to the security department for remedial actions.

- **Malfunction of a Smart Refrigerator.** A smart refrigerator could start ordering items already present, prompting the user to lodge a complaint with the vendor. The vendor investigates and determines that a sensor has malfunctioned. The refrigerator must then be replaced, and the incident and usage data must be recorded for further inquiry and remedial measures.

However, the peculiar nature of IoT incident response management results in some specific differences when compared to traditional, pre-IoT incident response management. Such specifics include the following:

- **Nature of IoT Networks.** IoT networks do not have uniform deployment attributes when compared with the traditional global Internet. A few IoT protocols address lightweight network nodes with ad hoc and mobile topologies. IoT access networks are vast amalgamations of different brands of nodes and network equipment. Such diversity will also continue to rise as more manufacturers join in.

- **Additional Safety Factors.** As IoT spreads into every walk of life, many untoward incidents are expected to affect personal safety. Such incidents could include the example mentioned above, in which a driverless cab is hacked. Another example could be the malfunction of a machine used to provide healthcare. This makes IoT incident management a very important aspect of the IoT landscape.

- **Dependence on Cloud.** With the critical role cloud plays in IoT, many IoT incidents can be traced back to cloud providers.

This raises issues of jurisdiction and control when addressing, investigating, and eradicating IoT incidents.

- **Vast Attack Surface.** IoT systems typically present a vast attack surface. With so many entities and such a widespread coverage area, attackers can more easily conduct reconnaissance and even generate small hacks with comparatively bigger impacts. For example, merely inputting incorrect or exaggerated data to sensors can disturb the overall system. IoT incident response management mechanisms must deal with these additional responsibilities to act swiftly, comprehensively, and with agility.

- **Highly constrained devices.** IoT comprises large numbers of *constrained devices*: lightweight entities with limited computing power, battery life, and memory. It is tough for constrained devices to form part of an incident response management chain that constantly generates, records, and transmits event logs. Therefore, IoT incident management at the access level requires special attention.

3. Phases of Incident Response Management in IoT

Incident response management is a phased process. Each phase must be carefully established for comprehensive and effective implementation. The process should start with the deployment of IoT infrastructure and continue as the network operates.

- **Preparatory Phase.** The process starts with planning for an incident response management mechanism. Generally, this phase begins with the inception of an IoT project.

- **Listening Watch Phase.** After planning comes implementation. In the listening watch phase, the mechanism is deployed over the IoT system for the purpose of constantly monitoring and detecting incidents within its area of responsibility.

- **Combat Phase.** The next phase involves combatting any incidents. Such combat includes making quick responses, corrective measures, and recovery from setbacks. This is the most difficult phase, especially in an IoT environment.

- **Aftershock Phase.** Finally, in the aftershock phase, some post-incident actions are performed. All affected IoT entities and services must be brought back to normal working conditions in a stable state.

In the following sections, we will explore each phrase in greater depth.

Preparatory Phase

The preparatory phase is the most important phase of incident response management. Preparation defines the scope, level, and goals of the overall system and dictates how seriously enterprise management treats proactive defense against cyberattacks.

3.1 Defining Scope

This includes answering the following questions:

- **What would be the scope of the system?** Should the proposed system cover only incidents happening within the enterprise, or is it intended to collaborate with other similar systems. If possible, incident response management should be linked with other such initiatives at higher and parallel levels. This would be beneficial to all involved parties.

- **At what levels should incident response management tentacles be placed?** Should the system cover all sites, offices, or zones within the organization, or will it just be a centralized system? For each incident management tentacle, 24/7 availability of resources would be required at those locations.

On the other hand, a strictly centralized mechanism would create single point of failure.

- **What is expected out of the incident response management system?** Cybersecurity, intended incident handling goals, and the preferred end state in case of a disaster or a minor incident should all be well documented.

3.2 Incident Categorization

Incidents must be categorized according to some classification. This makes it easier for the planning team to generate set response patterns against commonly occurring incidents. One intelligent classification method sorts incidents based on impact: low, moderate, high, or severe. When an incident is tagged according to its impact, the team can generate a set response. If proper classification of incidents is not in place, then every incident may generate chaos. Conversely, high-impact incidents may go unnoticed for quite some time.

In an IoT environment, impact can be measured either by the number of entities affected, the number and importance of processes or services disrupted, or both. Another realistic method can be to assign numbers against various attributes of the incidents and classify them based on their aggregate score.

3.3 Likely Set of Incidents

Preparing for IoT incident management should include hypothesizing threat scenarios beforehand. A prerequisite of threat scenario assessment is noting likely incident sets and preparing the incident response team to address them. Popular examples could include the following:

- Viruses or malware attacking IoT entities
- IoT web vulnerabilities leading to hacks
- DDoS attacks on IoT cloud services

- DDoS attacks launched using IoT entities
- Phishing and spear phishing attacks on users and entities
- Exploit kits[98] for IoT
- IoT WSAN attacks
- Traditional identity theft
- Cloud-based attacks

3.4 Liaison and Agreement with Cloud Provider

Because cloud is an essential part of IoT infrastructure, IoT incident response management must include cloud incident management. Separate incident handling mechanisms are required, but close coordination between both cloud and non-cloud incident handling mechanisms is necessary. Often, incidents in IoT access networks trace back to cloud providers as well. Without properly defined agreements with the cloud, IoT incident management is incomplete.

3.5 Building Team along with Infrastructure

During the planning phase, the incident response management team should be grown simultaneously with the infrastructure. Because the team should be familiar with the deployment pattern of the IoT project, it should either be involved in the deployment process from the outset, or it should revisit all deployment before starting its work. IoT deployment architecture is typically more complex than traditional projects.

The number of team members should depend on the scope of the incident management system, goals, sensitivity of the IoT project, and shift duration.

4. Listening Watch Phase

This phase deals with the monitoring and detection of incidents. Without detection, incidents cannot be handled in subsequent phases.

---

[98] A utility tool used to manage a variety of exploits.

4.1 SIEM Solution

Security incident and event management (SIEM) solutions have already gained a lot of popularity due to their effectiveness in detecting incidents. SIEM solutions continuously monitor the log files of network devices to identify any untoward incidents, by detecting unusual activities.

SIEM can be very helpful in handling and detecting IoT incidents. It can quickly analyze the logs of all IoT devices and nodes and identify unfamiliar activity. Wearable devices, smartphones, smart cars, and other IoT devices can all be augmented with SIEM software.

However, IoT's volume of traffic and number of entities challenge even advanced, modern SIEM solutions. Colossal volumes of logs must be considering when connecting entities with SIEM software. While its task is to filter incidents, even filtered IoT incidents might be too many. It would be nearly impossible for an administrator in an IoT project to read even the filtered logs during working hours. Therefore, present-day SIEM solutions need further refinement plus incident detection efficiency in preparation for the upcoming IoT boom.

4.2 Threat Scenarios

In addition to an efficient incident detection mechanism, it is equally necessary to consider relevant threat vectors. Realistic threat scenarios must be discussed and formulated during peacetime.

The IoT environment is relatively new, with many hypothetical threats. The threat of so many possible incidents is an envisioned difficulty with IoT incident response and management. Readymade threat scenarios make it easier for the team to ascertain a certain type of incident by correlation. Hypothesized IoT threat scenarios can be organized into a few example categories, including the following:

- Injection of malicious data from sensors
- Injection through spoofed addresses

- Stealing data through rogue devices
- Hacking attempts leading to privacy compromise
- Malware infections
- DDoS attacks
- Unauthorized access by compromising IAM
- Eavesdropping[99]
- Cloud-based attacks

4.3 Mock Exercises

Incident response management mock exercises provide another method to improve incident detection capabilities. Such exercises can be set up to play incidents in a test IoT environment with similar architecture to the real system. Entity hacking, DDoS attacks, masquerading entity addresses, cloud hacks, and similar incidents can be generated in the test environment. Associated detection capabilities can then be judged by evaluating the correctness of incident identification within a time frame.

5. Combat Phase

All preparation, planning, and exercising for threat scenarios are utilized in this phase, with the actual incident identified, reported, and addressed through the following process.

- Contain the incident from spreading further.
- Eradicate the incident by resolving the issue that caused it.
- Repair the damage done during the incident and recover the system to a stable state.

5.1 Incident Containment in IoT

With such a huge number of entities in IoT, incident containment is crucial. Generally, the best approach to stop the spread of an untoward

---

[99] Situation in which digital communications are intercepted by an unauthorized agent.

incident into the whole system is to remove the problematic entities as soon as possible. However, entities in doubt should also be removed and replaced. IoT entities are lightweight and, typically, are not costly. Therefore, choosing not to remove infected, or possibly infected, entities is rarely worth the risk.

5.2 Incident analysis and role of forensics in IoT

Incidents may be contained without sufficient analysis. However, for eradication and system recovery, proper incident analysis may be necessary.

IoT incident analysis can be tough, especially due to the large number of entities and dependency on cloud. However, by starting incident response planning at the conception of the IoT project, vendors could be required to provide necessary monitoring for their hardware in a common language. A comprehensive SIEM solution could manage the process and be deployed even before the entities are registered. No new entities that the existing SIEM solution cannot monitor should be purchased, due to any mismatches.

Another issue with incident analysis pertains to IoT forensics. Picking up investigative data from IoT entities can be difficult. With continuous data exchange among the huge number of IoT entities, incident traces and signatures are spread over a vast area. Therefore, efficient IoT forensic tools are critical for IoT incident response management.

5.3 Incident Recovery

Swift incident recovery is directly correlated to a proper understanding of the root causes of the incident and prior rehearsals. Proactive incident handling, while catering for maximum possible contingencies, typically results in a smooth recovery process. Otherwise, the process can be bumpy, turbulent, and much more time intensive.

In the IoT environment, incident management processes should be practiced, from start of occurrence until complete recovery. Regular practice when there are no problems will pay off when trouble comes. Prevention should be prioritized, but one must also know what to do when preventative measures fail.

6. The Aftershock Phase

After we contain the incident, eradicate the problems, and recover the system back to normal operation, the post-incident tasks arrive. This phase uses post-incident investigation and forensics to thoroughly analyze the basic reasons leading to the incidents. This includes a comprehensive inspection to determine whether the system has properly returned to its normal state after the recovery. Another important aspect after an incident is ascertaining losses, in terms of damage to the assets and loss of critical data.

Due to the varied entities and providers involved in IoT projects, incident reports should be shared laterally and vertically. This arrangement ensures better coordination and formidable defense against similar incidents reoccurring.

Also, because the IoT landscape is packed with hardware and software from different vendors, it is imperative to send the incident report to the concerned vendors. This may lead them to manufacture improved products in future.

Conclusion

Incident response management plays an important role in IoT-based solutions. Because IoT encompasses a colossal number of hardware and associated services, its incident detection, containment, eradication, recovery, and reporting capabilities affect its ability to provide sustained operation.

Since few current incident response management solutions are tailor-made for IoT, the field presents an open, interesting research area. New research can focus on IoT's large attack surface, as well as the increased number of stakeholders involved in IoT incident response management, compared with traditional incident handling. Other possible research opportunities could explore incident response team composition or SIEM solution refinement to support efficient incident response management.

IoT incident response setup and procedures should always begin at project inception. The procedures should then follow the planning and implementation stages of the overall IoT project. Prevention should be prioritized over mitigation, because mitigation is more complicated and will likely lead to at least some damage remaining.

Printed in the United States
By Bookmasters